MW01131826

Study Guide: A *Macbeth* Commentary

Other WordSmith Study Guides:

A *Hamlet* Commentary
A *King Lear* Commentary
An *Othello* Commentary
Writing Unseen Commentaries: A Student Help Book
Reading Between the Lines: A Student Help Book
Persuasion: A Workbook Edition
The Prologue to the Canterbury Tales: A Workbook Edition

Contact email: wordsmith@litworks.com

'As I did stand my watch upon the hill,
I look'd toward Birnam, and anon, methought,
The wood began to move.' (V v)

FOREWORD

To Teachers

Our notes for students (below) explain how the Commentary can support them in their exam preparation. Beyond its applicability to assessment demands within particular programmes of study, however, it will help students develop a more general and long-lasting understanding of how literature, and words within literature, 'work'.

As part of that process it introduces students to a simple analytical tool (SCASI – Setting, Character, Action, Style and Ideas) designed to help them think about works of literature in an organised way.

Two further suggestions:

o   Be selective, if time constraints make that appropriate. Use the Commentary only for key scenes and passages.
o   Vary your use of the resource. Teaching from it 'live', for instance, (in class and orally), can be very effective.

To Students

Here is a list of the ways this Commentary can help you, and some suggestions about how to use it.

First step

Read the play – there is no substitute for that!

Some ways in which you can read it (you can combine methods) are:

o   In class

o   By yourself, using a good edition (one which explains the unusual words and phrases)

o   Aloud, in a group, either in or out of school, with or without a teacher. This will bring the play alive for you and will allow you to discuss the meaning of its more difficult parts.

o   While listening to an audio tape. This will help you focus on the words of the text.

o   Alongside a video version. (Read a scene, watch it; or watch a scene then read it; or watch the whole play then read the whole play; or the other way around.)

o   Alongside this Commentary.

What the Commentary does

o   It explores what's 'really' happening in each scene – what the situation is, why the characters are speaking and behaving the way they are, and how the play is moving forward.

o   More importantly, it asks why Shakespeare is *making* things happen in that particular way.

o   It is specifically designed to help you prepare for the passage-based commentary questions in A Level and AP exams, and the Individual Oral Commentary part of the IB Diploma course: it draws your attention to the kind of things you will be expected to say about individual passages. In addition, it has sample commentary questions, advice on how to prepare a passage-based commentary, and a specimen commentary.

o   All the way through the Commentary, and especially in the Student Response sections, essay questions are used as a way of exploring the play further, and also as a means of encouraging you to think about *Macbeth* not only as an exam text and a piece of working theatre, but also as a literary work of great significance.

o   It explains the troublesome words and ideas when they are especially important or interesting.

o   It is set up to be used with your copy of the play. Line references are given in the margin of the Commentary to make it easier for you to move from one to the other. (References differ from one edition of the play to another, but not by very much.)

o   The Overview section for each scene lists other, broader points of interest, under useful headings which will help you when you come to revise.

o   The Student Response sections record some of the things students have said about the play, about the difficulties in staging it and the issues raised by it – ambition, loyalty, betrayal, illusion and delusion, manhood and womanhood, the right to rule, the difficulty of changing direction in our lives, revenge, justice…

CONTENTS

Act One Scene One	Commentary	1
	Overview	2
	Student Response	3
Act One Scene Two	Commentary	4
	Overview	7
	Student Response	8
Act One Scene Three	Commentary	9
	Overview	14
	Student Response	16
Act One Scene Four	Commentary	18
	Overview	19
	Student Response	20
Act One Scene Five	Commentary	21
	Overview	25
	Student Response	26
Act One Scene Six	Commentary	28
	Overview	28
	Student Response	29
Act One Scene Seven	Commentary	30
	Overview	34
	Student Response	34
	Additional Essay Questions (A Level)	35
	Commentary Practice – General	35
	Practice Commentary 1	37
	Model Commentary	40
	Commentary – Further Suggestions	42
Act Two Scene One	Commentary	43
	Overview	46
	Student Response	46
Act Two Scene Two	Commentary	48
	Overview	50
	Student Response	50
Act Two Scene Three	Commentary	52
	Overview	56
	Student Response	57
Act Two Scene Four	Practice Commentary 2	59
	Additional Essay Questions (A Level)	63
	A Level Questions: An Overview	64
Act Three Scene One	Commentary	66
	Overview	69

	Student Response	70
Act Three Scene Two	Commentary	72
	Overview	74
	Student Response	75
Act Three Scene Three	Commentary	76
	Overview	76
	Student Response	77
Act Three Scene Four	Commentary	78
	Overview	83
	Student Response	83
Act Three Scene Five	Commentary	85
	Overview	85
	Student Response	86
Act Three Scene Six	Commentary	87
	Overview	88
	Student Response	89
	Additional Essay Questions (A Level)	89
	Practice Commentary 3	90
Act Four Scene One	Commentary	91
	Overview	96
	Student Response	97
Act Four Scene Two	Commentary	98
	Overview	100
	Student Response	101
Act Four Scene Three	Commentary	103
	Overview	109
	Student Response	110
	Additional Essay Questions (A Level)	110
	Commentary Practice 4	111
Act Five Scene One	Commentary	112
	Overview	114
	Student Response	114
Act Five Scene Two	Commentary	116
	Overview	118
	Student Response	118
Act Five Scene Three	Commentary	119
	Overview	121
	Student Response	122
Act Five Scene Four	Commentary	123
	Overview	123
	Student Response	124

Act Five Scene Five   Commentary   125
                                 Overview   128
                                 Student Response   128

Act Five Scene Six   Commentary   130
                                 Overview   130
                                 Student Response   130

Act Five Scene Seven   Commentary   131
                                 Overview   132
                                 Student Response   132

Act Five Scene Eight   Commentary   133
                                 Overview   134
                                 Student Response   135

Act Five Scene Nine   Commentary   137
                                 Overview   137
                                 Student Response   137
                                 Practice Commentary 5   138
                                 Additional Essay Questions (A Level)   139

Further Essay Questions (International Baccalaureate)   140

Further Essay Questions (A Level)   141

Advanced Placement Free-Response Questions   142

Commentary 'Help' Pages   143

Final Words   144

Macbeth – **A Study Commentary**

Act One

Act One Scene One

Commentary

This is one of Theatre's best-known opening scenes. Some commentators have argued that it's redundant. Look, however, at some of the things it does for the audience.

Principally, it gives us an idea of the play's overall context, the background against which events are going to unfold.

What significant impressions of the play's context, and the forces at work there, do we gain from each of the following?

o   The thunder and lightning
o   The fact that there are *three* witches
o   The fact that they're making plans   *1*
o   Their sing-song style of speech
o   The way they speak in strict turns
o   The phrase *hurly-burly*   *3*
o   The idea that a battle can be both lost and won   *4*
o   The information that this battle will soon be over   *5*
o   The mention of Macbeth's name with no indication of who he is   *7*
o   The calling of the Witches' familiars   *8-9*
o   The idea that fair things can be foul and vice-versa   *10*
o   The reference to fog and filthy air   *11*

---

o   Turmoil and conflict are in the air.
o   The magic number: supernatural power is abroad.
o   Those supernatural forces are busy and *organised.*
o   Evidence of ritual – and of the Witches' enjoyment in what they are doing
o   Ritual again – and cooperative power
o   It indicates that there are more important things happening than the fighting to which they refer. '*Hurly-burly*' is a dismissive term: the battle is reduced in the Witches' scheme of things to the dimensions of a playground squabble.
o   In the end, everything balances out.
o   It's not the battle itself which matters, but the things which will follow.
o   They have been talking about him – he is central to their plans.
o   The Witches have other business to attend to '*anon*' (immediately).
o   Things in the world are not what they seem, and values can be turned upside down.
o   It's difficult to see things clearly; and the very air we breathe can be poisonous.

All in all a pretty ominous account of the world in which Macbeth lives.

We've focussed on the fine detail of the scene in order to give you some idea of how closely you're going to have to examine the text of the play. Just about every word (other than the ands and buts, and sometimes even they) can tell us something useful about what Shakespeare is trying to do in a particular passage. If you're unhappy at the thought of going through the play as slowly as that, don't be:

- o You may find the process more interesting than you think, particularly if you come to see it as a kind of treasure hunt in which you are seeking out valuable ideas.
- o It's excellent practice for the precise analysis you'll need to perform in other parts of your Literature course (Unseen Commentary/Rhetorical Analysis particularly).
- o You can if you wish concentrate only on the key passages, the ones which are more likely to come up in an exam.

Overview: other things to note

When you're working close to the printed text like that, however, you can lose sight of the play...so it's a good idea to step back and pay attention to some of the larger aspects of each scene before you move on. The headings below will help you do that – the first five represent common aspects of nearly all plays and novels, and much poetry.

Just to demonstrate the system, we've rearranged under this set of headings some of the notes on the significant features of *Scene One* we made above. You'll find the scheme much more useful when we deal with the longer scenes.

Setting (*'where the story happens'. There are different kinds of setting – geographical, historical, social, economic, philosophical*)
- o The sense of place Shakespeare establishes, not by including physical details but by giving us some idea of what sort of world this is and what matters to the Witches

Character (*who the people in the story are and why they do what they do. Characterisation – the methods the dramatist uses to help us see his characters clearly – is also important*)
- o The Witches'
  - confidence
  - omniscience: they know when the battle will end and where they will find Macbeth.
  - focus
  - enjoyment
- o Macbeth's centrality

Action (*'what happens', and the way the story is told*)
- o The early sense of foreboding
- o The feeling that there are strong forces at work
- o The scene's crispness
- o The way Shakespeare prepares us for the next scene on *'the heath' (line 6)* before sunset

Style (*the words and images characters and Shakespeare choose, and how they are put together for particular purposes*)
- o Incantation, with its strict rhythm and mystical overtones
- o Question and answer – part of the patterning of the speech
- o Alliteration (*'set...sun; fair...foul...fog...filthy'*)
- o Reference by name to the familiars Paddock and Graymalkin – adds 'authenticity' to the Witches' characters.
- o Tight structure and order of speaking (suggesting control, efficiency)
- o Economy (the Witches waste neither time nor words).

Ideas (*which, when they recur, become the play's themes*):
- o The deceitfulness of appearance
- o The difficulty of knowing (seeing) anything with certainty

<u>General</u> *(anything else of interest, particularly how the play works as a play)*

o Plays (mostly) tell stories. The stories begin with 'situations'. People like their lives to be stable and as far as possible enjoyable. A situation arises when something happens to threaten stability or enjoyment. That something may have already taken place by the time the play begins, or it may occur during the opening scenes. The rest of the play tells the story of how the situation is resolved (the problem is sorted out) and stability, with the possibility of enjoyment, restored.

This play opens with news of a battle being fought (nearby? That would explain the *'filthy air', line 11*). A battle would certainly qualify as a 'situation'! So the stability of someone's life, and presumably their enjoyment, have been disrupted. Will both of those be re-established once the battle is over? Probably not – the battle is only the beginning of things as far as the Witches are concerned. Will they ever be re-established? Ah, that's a question to be answered by the story we've come to the theatre to be told.

Student Response

The class have had some fun with the potentially comic aspects of the opening scene. (How do the Witches *'hover'* off the stage at the end?) I've told them about an amateur production I saw in the Caribbean which had only one (male) witch delivering the whole of the scene himself (it was a small-scale production) directly underneath a single spotlight. A dog wandered in from outside (it was a fairly informal theatre), sat at his feet and howled throughout. Partly comic, but eerie also…

'Is this scene supposed to be frightening?'

'If you believed in witches you might find it frightening. People in Shakespeare's day did believe in them. Women were killed for being witches.'

'And what about the idea that things can turn out to be the opposite of what you thought? Isn't that frightening, in a different sort of way?'

There's plenty of agreement from the class, and some interesting personal examples.

It's a bit early to be thinking about essay questions, I tell them; but in an examination they might find themselves faced with one which reads something like:

> *Discuss the opening scenes of plays you have studied, and show how, in them, playwrights have worked to arouse audience interest in the story to follow.*

They should be able to make some useful notes in response to that, even from a scene as short as this one.

*****

Act One Scene Two

Commentary

War is a bloody business. The Captain's *'plight'* (injury) reminds us that lives are being lost close at hand.   2

The Captain's main dramatic purpose is to establish Macbeth as a hero. But Shakespeare uses him also to add suspense to the scene. He does that by a kind of trick. The Captain is ordered to,

> *'Say to the King the knowledge of the broil,*   6-7
> **As thou didst leave it.'**

He begins, however, a little bit earlier in the story, at a point where the outcome is far from decided:

> *'Doubtful it stood.'*   7

He can thus tell the tale as it happened, revealing only in *line 22* that Macbeth has killed Macdonwald.

So Shakespeare makes the most of the Captain's tale. An exam question which would allow you to use a detail like that might read,

> *'Plays are much shorter than novels. Narrative economy must therefore be one of the dramatist's main concerns.'*
>
> *Show how Shakespeare, in 'Macbeth', practices the principle of dramatic economy.*

Look out for other examples of the multiple use, for dramatic effect, of minor characters and what they say: it's the mark of a skilful playwright.

There is a clear division in the Captain's tale between the 'good' and 'bad' people in the conflict. The good people are the ones on our side, and all the others are bad. That's what happens in war – we see things in simple black and white. Macdonwald is therefore described as *'merciless'* (that may mean   9
undeserving of mercy rather than lacking it) and a *'slave' (line 20)* while Macbeth is *'brave'* and   16,19
'Valour's minion'.

Note the role of Fortune, however: she seems to be on Macdonwald's side but betrays him. People may   14-15
be easy to categorise, but the forces which control our lives are more difficult to read. (The whole story shows of course that people are just as opaque, after all.)

So the Captain presents Macbeth as a superman, on the 'good' side. A mark of that stature is his
readiness to scorn one universal force (Fortune) and embrace another (Valour). In other words he is   16-20
unwilling to trust his luck and relies instead on his courage. That's a not unexpected characteristic of a
'hero'; but the weightiness of the figurative language (both Fortune and Valour are personified) makes
Macbeth appear larger than life. That becomes important when we consider the question of what a
'tragic hero' is.

Here's a somewhat tongue-in-cheek essay question (not to be tackled, at least not yet):

> *'The bigger they are the harder they fall.'*
>
> *Relate that common saying to the downfall of a central figure in a play you have studied.*

Just how much larger than life is Macbeth, and in what ways? And does his 'size' change as the story moves through its various stages? That will be an ongoing question for us.

Even at this early stage, however (we've yet to meet him), we can find signs that he may be more than a conventional hero. He has *'carv'd out his passage'* to Macdonwald. Is there a suggestion in that *19* phrase that for him war is something of an art, allowing creative as well as destructive acts? And then we hear that he did not shake hands with nor say goodbye to Macdonwald *'Till he unseam'd him from the nave to th'chops'*. Maybe there's a subtle indication in *'Till'* that once he had killed Mcdonwald he *22* did in fact shake hands (with the *'unseam'd'* body) and perhaps even said farewell to the head on the battlements. The grim humour of such actions would not be out of line with Macbeth's character as it appears later.

'Unseam'd' is worth a further note. It's one of a series of tailoring images in the play. But it may also be a pun: can you see how if it were spelt *'unseem'd'* it might tie in with the idea that things aren't always what they appear to be?

> It *seemed* as if Fortune was on Macdonwald's side, but Macbeth dispelled that illusion with his sword.

Note *'our'* battlements: trophies are important…and the beheading itself looks forward to Macbeth's *23* own end (apologies if that's a 'spoiler).

Duncan's exclamations are designed mainly to let the Captain (and the audience) draw breath. But we *24* are reminded in *'cousin'* that Macbeth was related to Duncan (they shared the same grandfather); and in *'gentleman'* that heroic behaviour was expected in one of high birth. Both exclamations therefore help to clarify the play's value-systems.

There's a fair example of dramatic irony at the beginning of the Captain's next speech. The general meaning of *lines 25-28* is that further trouble can come our way just when we've escaped the last lot. In the narrow context of the battle what that means is that no sooner had Macbeth won some relief by killing Macdonwald than the Norwegian forces saw their chance and attacked (maybe from the East, where the sun rises – *''gins his reflection'* – and from which direction they had travelled to Scotland anyway). In the wider context of the play…well, what?

> If you already know the outline of the story you may see how that general statement about danger arising in quarters from which have just received succour becomes significant for Duncan's situation. (Think about what Macbeth has just done for him and what he is about to do *to* him.)

Don't assume that Shakespeare planned it this way, that he's deliberately laying a trail of 'clues for the discerning theatregoer' about what's going to happen.

'Playwrights seek to make the patterns of existence visible to their audiences.'

Show how playwrights you have studied attempt to do this.

That's all Shakespeare is doing here. One of the 'patterns of existence' is life's ability to deal us a second blow when we're just recovering from a first one, and to deal it moreover from the least-expected direction. Think again about Duncan, the faith he places in Macbeth, and how it is rewarded. That's irony for you. It's what we call *dramatic* irony here because what is said (by the Captain) takes on a much greater significance (one of which he can't possible be aware as he speaks) in the light of later events.

And maybe it's an overstatement to say that Shakespeare is doing it or attempting to do it. Life's ironies and its other patterns are only too good at revealing themselves. All Shakespeare has to do is tell the story.

An important part of the account of the battle (as it's told by the Captain) is how both justice and valour helped Macbeth drive off the *'skipping kerns'*; and a further irony in the larger story is that Macbeth's murder of Duncan is both unjust (in its motives) and cowardly (in its manner).

30

Duncan acts as the prompter here, again breaking up for us the long account of the battle; but he is also the king, and he does have the power of reward, and the eagerness with which he asks for details of the battle foreshadows the eagerness with which he honours the man who more than any other ensured its success for him. Dramatic economy once more. And dramatic irony.

33-34

The comparison of the second attack with a storm which arises unexpectedly (*lines 24-25* above) could be termed an epic simile (a long comparison designed to aggrandise the thing described). The Captain now offers two more. They aren't in fact very long, but they are significant for their associations. The first one is particularly pointed. Eagles are not normally afraid of hawks, nor lions of hares. (Macbeth and Banquo were just as unafraid of the Norwegians, is what the Captain is saying.) That if you like is one of the 'patterns of existence' we have been talking about: it's 'the way things are'. But the way things are can change, the normal structures and relationships of life can be disrupted. So we will find a very similar image in *Act Two*, one of a series in which an Old Man describes the unnatural events which have followed Duncan's murder (itself an unnatural act):

> *'On Tuesday last,*
> *A falcon, towering in her pride of place,*
> *Was by a mousing owl hawked at, and killed.'*
> *(Act Two Scene Four lines 11-13)*

Why do we mention that now? Because a play is held together in part by its echoes (and its images) and we need to learn to listen for them. Essay question:

> *Show how dramatists can use a variety of methods to bind their plays into a cohesive and shapely whole. Illustrate your answer from a play or plays you have studied.*

Even if you're delivering a commentary rather than writing an essay, the examiner will be particularly impressed if you offer some cross-references like that.

Shakespeare keeps Duncan at the centre of things. He commends the Captain and orders that his wounds be attended to. He notes the arrival of Ross and Angus, asks them for more news, expresses relief when they give it to him and dispenses justice and reward to the Thane of Cawdor and Macbeth respectively. If upheaval in the established order is to be one of the themes of the play, Shakespeare must show how well-established that order is at the beginning of the story: the King is the King.

He also makes the most of whatever suspense remains in the military situation. Lenox describes the newcomers as being clearly in a hurry to speak; and Shakespeare then uses something of the same device he employed in the Captain's earlier narrative: Ross employs the present tense when he begins –

47

> *'The Norweyan banners **flout** the sky'* –

51

as if the matter is not yet settled. But it is.

Shakespeare also emphasises the odds against Macbeth in order to make his eventual victory seem the greater. Pick out three or four details in *lines 50-55* which have that effect.

> o   The Norwegian banners seem to mock Duncan's forces.
> o   The Norwegian king himself leads the attack.
> o   He has a large force of men.
> o   He is assisted by the Thane of Cawdor.
> o   The conflict he initiates is *'dismal'* (ominous, frightening).

Now note the methods Shakespeare uses in *lines 56-59* to explain and celebrate Macbeth's victory.

> o   Macbeth is described as having married (i.e. become allied to) the mythical Roman goddess of war.
> o   He is protected by armour which has been put to the proof, i.e. well tested.
> o   He matches the king of Norway man for man, weapon for weapon, strength for strength.

'Lavish' is interesting. It's explained by most editors as meaning something like 'insolent' or 'excessive'. Both of those terms and some of the others that have been offered suggest behaviour beyond what is acceptable or normal and therefore threatening to the natural order of things. That theme again.

The idea of balance in events is reinforced in the final line of the scene, with its antithesis (Cawdor's loss set against Macbeth's gain) and rhyme (*'won'* and *'done'*). What is ironical, however, is the false air of finality both the antithesis and the rhyme – and the act of reward itself – impart. This is the beginning, not the end, of a 'situation'.

Overview: other things to note

Setting
o   The distance of this place from where the important events are happening. Macbeth is in the thick of things, Duncan isn't.

Character
o   Use of minor characters (the Captain, Lenox, Ross)
o   Duncan's characterlessness: he is the King, no less; but he is no more, either.
o   Mention of Banquo as one who fought alongside Macbeth and showed almost equal valour. The foundation is laid for the account of their very important relationship.

Action
o   The ironic patterning of things once more. '*That* Thane of Cawdor' will no longer be in a position to betray Duncan, but the new one will.
o   The speed with which the scene is wrapped up. There are more important things awaiting our attention than the matter of who has won the fight.

Style
o   The dramatic simplicity of Duncan's opening question *(line 1)* in contrast to the formality of his second sentence (note the inversion of the phrases). War is two things – at a personal level it is horribly destructive; at a public, or political, level it is a massive and impersonal event.
o   Echoes, in the storm imagery *(lines 25-6)*, of the thunder and lightning of *Scene One*

<u>Ideas</u>

o   Appearance and reality (*'seemeth', line 2* – nothing should be taken at face value).
o   Loyalty and heroism (*'the Sergeant /Who like a good and worthy soldier, fought /'Gainst my captivity' – Hail, brave friend!', lines 3-5*)
o   The irony of war: when two armies are well-matched they can destroy each other and neither ends up as the victor. Both will drown *(lines 8-9).*
o   Justice, reward
o   A man's worth and how it is judged – here, by what he has done

<u>General</u>

o   The early conflict in the play, and the physical form it takes. A fairly basic essay question would be:

> *'Drama is conflict.' Is this too simplistic a view? Discuss it in relation your chosen play(s).*

The straightforward way of tackling that would be to list the different types of conflict (internal, political, emotional and so on) to be found in the play(s) you're writing about, and then to discuss what's left over – the important things which are *not* conflict. (You could then probably demonstrate that it *is* a simplistic statement, because:

- 'conflict' can mean different things.
- there are some important items left over, e.g. 'universal truths', 'ideas about human nature', 'surprise').

Student Response

'Why doesn't Duncan fight his own battles?'

'I reckon it's because Shakespeare wants Macbeth to be at the centre of things from the beginning.'

'I think he also needs to give a reason why King Duncan owes him.'

*****

'Why is the story of the battle told by two different people?'

'Maybe to add some suspense – the Sergeant tells us all he knows, then Ross comes in and tells us more.'

'Why doesn't Angus have anything to say, then?'

'The Captain and Ross have probably told us everything Shakespeare needs us to know about the battle.'

*****

The questions could have led to a wider discussion, or even an essay question:

> *Sometimes what happens off stage, or has happened before the play begins, is as important as what takes place during the course of the visible action in the present. By what methods and how successfully, in the plays you have studied, do dramatists let us know about off-stage or previous events?*

The important thing for the moment, however, is that the class are beginning to answer questions with, 'Because Shakespeare…'

*****

Act One Scene Three

Commentary

In *Scene One* the Witches seemed to have a choice about the conditions they would next meet under (*'thunder, lightning or...rain'*). We now find that they have chosen thunder, and its noise serves to announce their entrance. The arrival shortly of Macbeth and Banquo is marked by a drum, and editors have puzzled over why...but the contrast between the power of the thunder and the beating of what need not be a very impressive drum could have some dramatic impact.

The first part of this scene reinforces much of what was conveyed by the play's opening scene. Try to find examples from *lines 1-36* of some of the same things (slight changes of wording have been necessary).

o   Turmoil and conflict in the air
o   The magic number 3
o   Evidence that the supernatural forces are busy and *organised*
o   Ritual
o   The Witches' enjoyment
o   Their cooperative power
o   The sense that they are marking time until they can take events forward
o   Scorn for the affairs of men and women
o   The idea of scores being settled and of things cancelling each other out
o   The fact that the Witches have other business to attend to
o   The idea that things in the world are not what they seem, and values can be turned upside down

---

o   The thunder, and the storms at sea
o   *Lines 35-36*
o   The Witches' accounts of what they have been up to; and their speed of travel *(line 33)*
o   *Lines 32-37*
o   *'I'll do, and I'll do, and I'll do...Look what I have...A drum! a drum! /Macbeth doth come.'*
o   *'I'll give thee a wind...and I another.'*
o   They are mainly gossiping while they wait for Macbeth.
o   *'rump-fed ronyon'*; and the First Witch in her sieve is more than a match for the captain in his fine ship *The Tyger*.
o   She will make him *'dwindle, peak and pine'* in contrast to his fat wife.
o   The plans they are laying
o   The sailor's wife thought she was dealing only with an old woman.

This part of the scene also looks forward, however.
o   Macbeth also will be made to pay a price for something he has done.
o   He will be drained dry as hay (spiritually), and will shrink (*'dwindle'*) in stature.
o   He and his wife will both be denied sleep, and will live as a man *'forbid'* (cursed).

We should note that there are limitations to the Witches' power: they are not allowed to actually sink *The Tyger*. Two points of interest arise.
o   Macbeth's *'bark'* (the ship of his life) does in fact founder...but he clearly sinks it himself.
o   He uses the Witches' omnipotence as an excuse for doing what he does – they have decreed his kingship, he says, and he must go along with that. But we note here that they are not omnipotent...

'Foul and fair' again, with a similar underlying idea (do you remember what that was?)   *38*

9

> There's a choice, really: either things can be
> o   both fair and foul (this day is fair because of their victory but also foul because of the weather)
> or they can
> o   appear to be fair and turn out to be foul.
>
> The first idea is more appropriate here; the second one points again to a more fundamental theme in the play.

Macbeth and Banquo think this is a chance meeting. We know that it is not.   *39*

The physical details Banquo gives of the Witches' appearance makes them seem: *40-47*
o   more mysterious?
o   more believable?
o   more repulsive?
o   more frightening?
o   more world-worn ('*withered*') and therefore more knowing?

The Witches speak formally once more. They make a distinction between the man himself *('All hail')*   *48-50*
and each of the titles *('hail to thee, Thane of Glamis')* he has acquired or is about to acquire. A man is
more than the things he owns. The question at the end of every tragedy is: what of the man is left when
all of his trappings have been taken away? We'll ask that question about Macbeth, in our discussion of
Act Five.

Why *does* Macbeth '*start*'?   *51*

Things go in threes – the Witches are still a trio, of course; and the patterning of Macbeth's present and
future status is underlined by the way Banquo phrases his comment to the Witches: '*present
grace...noble having...royal hope*'.   *55-56*

'*Rapt*' is worth a mention, particularly since Banquo uses it again in a moment *(line 142)*. Its simplest   *57*
meaning is 'withdrawn in thought'; but beyond that it carries the idea that the thinker has been seized
by something (as in 'raptor' - here, by the thoughts the Witches have put in Macbeth's mind) and is in
a state of 'rapture' (entrancement, with some supernatural overtones). Then there's the possibility of a
further meaning overlay in 'wrapped' (which would make it a pun, with the suggestion that Macbeth is
wrapping, or cloaking, his thoughts from the outside world). Even short and apparently simple
words....

Banquo's view of the Witches is different from Macbeth's (and see the additional notes under
<u>Character</u> below). As far as he is concerned they are no more than seers, and maybe not even that *('If
you can look into the sands of time')*; they may have the ability to predict the future but cannot control   *58*
it. Contrast that with Macbeth's later willingness to believe that since they know the future they will
also be instrumental in bringing their predictions to pass *'without my stir', line 144*.

The Witches offer Banquo no titles: he is what he is. They speak to him in riddles, and riddles play on   *62-69*
word definitions...which in turn, here, depend on the values you choose to apply – to, for instance, the
question of what happiness, or greatness, are.

Macbeth begins and ends his next speech with commands, and there are three questions sandwiched   *70,78*
between them. The Witches answer none of the questions and obey neither order. He should have been
warned: the forces at play in his life from now on will not do his bidding.

The next two short speeches from Banquo then Macbeth should be read as pair: they are nearly identical in length, in style, in structure, in what they say. The contrast lies in their final parts. Banquo shows his curiosity only – *'Whither are they vanished?'* while Macbeth reveals his total engagement with what they have told him, and his passion to hear more – *'Would they had stayed!'* Shakespeare thus, by the very design of those four lines, points up the difference between the two men, a difference which will increase until one hurls the other into the chasm which has opened up between them.

80

82

For the moment they are friends, musing over what they have heard, comparing notes. Comparing promises? Each seems more interested in what the other may gain. Is there jealousy and insecurity here, if only in one direction?

86-88

'Went it not so?': the Witches delivered their news by means of something approaching an incantation, a chant if you like, akin to a song. That explains Macbeth's rather odd phrase here, as if he trying to recall a melody. But what he has heard has been music to his ears in another sense, and he's trying to recapture the magic of it. We can imagine, however, that when Banquo takes up the image *('To the selfsame tune and words')* he is poking mild fun at his friend. The whole thing has mattered much less to him.

The timing of Ross's and Angus's arrival is perfect (dramatically). The phrase 'Thane of Cawdor' is still hanging in the air. We know what news Ross and Angus bring; and Shakespeare makes us wait just long enough for it to be delivered. The formality and elaborate stiffness of Ross's opening speech becomes almost a frustration to us. That effect is deliberate, and Shakespeare achieves it by depicting Duncan as virtually frozen in indecision between expressing his admiration for Macbeth and rewarding him – a somewhat artificial state, described in artificial (and 'official') language.

88

There are some ironies and other fine touches tucked away in this turgid (pompous) verse, however. The struggle in Duncan as to how he should respond to Macbeth's heroism is a pale foreshadowing of the struggle which will take place inside Macbeth as he decides whether or not to kill Duncan. Duncan is *'silenc'd'* temporarily by his internal debate; he will be silenced forever as an outcome of Macbeth's. Ross's actual phrasing – *'Which should be thine or his'* – points to the question soon to exercise Macbeth: what, of Duncan's, can he make his own?

93

Probably the most telling image in the passage is one which hardly seems to have a place there: *'Strange images of death'* is too strong, too original, too apposite a word-picture for this laboured communication. The remainder of the play will be filled with strange images of death, most of them created by Macbeth himself; but this forehint of the horrors to come is too rich – it is overpowered and overpowering in this context.

97

The ironies continue. *'For an earnest of a greater honour'* can only make Macbeth think of that greatest honour of all which the Witches have promised him. And anything which reminds us of his beginning ambition and incipient treachery will underscore the irony of this speech. In praising Macbeth Duncan is looking forward unwittingly to his own death at the hands of the very man he is seeking to reward.

104

Ross's *'Hail'*, of course, echoes the Witches', and strengthens the connection between what Macbeth has (just) been given and what he was (earlier) promised.

106

Who is Banquo speaking to here? His question (more of an exclamation in fact) would mean nothing to Ross and Angus. What does the word *'devil'* tell us about Banquo's feelings towards the Witches now?

107

'Borrowed robes': Macbeth is not implying that Cawdor's robes (title) will not fit him, just that they aren't his to wear (yet). Clothing images later in the play, however, do imply that Macbeth does not properly fill the role of king. Look out for them.

109

Banquo may have spoken the words, *'What, can the devil speak true!'* as an aside; Macbeth now without doubt says things he would not want even Banquo to hear. This is the beginning of his departure from his friend.
116-117

But the beginning distance between them breeds suspicion, and he attempts to probe Banquo's thoughts. Macbeth has already moved in his imaginings to a time when he will in fact be king: why would Banquo's sons rather than his (Macbeth's) not succeed him? Even before he has gained the kingship he has begun to worry about losing it.
118-120

Banquo seems to know what is in *Macbeth's* mind. *'Enkindle'* implies that Macbeth has it in him to burn with an ambition for kingship. But Banquo is still Macbeth's friend, and feels a need to warn him. The powers of evil, he says (he seems to have placed the Witches, finally, in that category) tell us things which are true but less important so that we come to trust what they say: they then mislead us massively into actions which produce terrible results. The important thing about the title Macbeth has just been granted is not that it is a trifle (although it's interesting that Banquo describes it as such) but that it is *'honest'*, i.e. gained honestly as well as real. The *'deepest consequence'* into which we are betrayed has less to do with the importance of kingship (in comparison with Thanedom) and more with the dimensions of what Macbeth would have to do to get it.
121
124
125,126

Banquo seems to have thought that through as rapidly as Macbeth, and has even gone beyond him. He now takes Ross and Angus aside. The theatrical reason for that is that it allows Macbeth to reveal his secret thoughts to the audience. But there has to be another justification, one which makes sense within the play: Banquo must have a reason as well as Shakspeare. Does he want to share his growing concern about Macbeth? Surely not – he could not do that without setting off all sorts of alarm bells. He does draw Ross's and Angus's attention to Macbeth's enrapture *(line 142)*; but then he makes excuses for him *(lines 144-146)*. Remember this little episode when Lady Macbeth tries to cover up for Macbeth after he has seen Banquo's ghost and acts even more strangely...
127

See also the later reference to this speech of Banquo's (<u>'Character</u>... o Inner conflict', page 14).

Macbeth does not seem to have listened to Banquo's warning. He has been carried away by a vision of himself as the central figure in a glorious play. The play's prologue has just been delivered and in it he has been pronounced Thane of both Glamis and Cawdor. The main part of the play will tell how he becomes king. The very thing that Banquo tried to caution him about – the *'trifles'* which the instruments of darkness use to ensnare us – Macbeth seizes on as proof that the play may become a reality and he will be crowned king.

'Swelling act': an acknowledgment perhaps (Shakespeare the dramatist showing through) of the shape of a well-made play, which 'swells' towards its climax.
127

See also the detailed analysis later of the elements of conflict in this speech ('Character...o Inner conflict', page 14). Note now, however, the antitheses – balanced statements – of the passage and how the oppositions in it are reflected in the sentence structure: *lines 131, 131-137, 137-138, 140-141, 141-142* – one example of antithesis in each. Good practice!

There are other things of note in the speech.
o The *'horrid image'* (of a murdered Duncan) – one of the *'strange images of death'* to be found in the play. Ross has just said *(lines 95-96)* that Macbeth was clearly not afraid of the images of death he created on the battlefield; Macbeth is terrified of the one he has now created in his mind.
135
o Macbeth's *'function'* (ability to act) is almost smothered in *'surmise'* (speculation) even more devastatingly when he hesitates before killing Duncan in the pivotal speech *'Is this a dagger that I see before me?'*, Act Two Scene One.
140-141
Macbeth does badly want to be king; but he also badly wants to avoid any responsibility for what that

might take. He sees the Witches as the instruments of Chance (or Fate – the two terms overlap) and hopes that whatever needs to be done to put him on the throne, they will do. This short speech also, then, looks forward to his moment of indecision outside Duncan's bedroom, when he finally accepts that if he does not perform the act of murder, no-one will.

143

Here's another of the clothing images. Macbeth will not give himself any time at all to become accustomed to his new title (Thane of Cawdor) before he seizes and puts on the larger garment of kingship. And that larger garment will never sit well on him.

144-146

The next line and a half aren't as straightforward as they might appear, and have been interpreted differently by different editors. They're best read as if they offer two separate statements (both attempts by Macbeth to make himself feel better about things – he has been deeply disturbed by the Witches' prophecy).

146-147

o   'Come what come may': let things happen as they will (Macbeth once more shows his unwillingness to act in his own interests).
o   Time and the hour runs through the roughest day: either
    • Even the worst of days comes to an end (but that doesn't altogether make sense – this has in some ways been a very good day for him), or
    • A time and an hour for action will come, nomatter what the difficulties (Macbeth does within this explanation seem to hold out the possibility that he will take things into his own hands – when the time is right).

Which interpretation of the second statement do you think is more accurate?

(It's fine in an exam, by the way, to say that something is ambiguous – capable of being understood in more than one way; and if you think there isn't enough evidence to allow us to make up our minds about it, say that. The examiner will be impressed that you're aware of the possibilities and also willing to keep an open mind. Literary criticism or commentary is rarely about finding the 'right' answer).

'Worthy Macbeth': irony of a slightly different kind, not so much dramatic irony (which rests in events and the contradictions between them) as in words (when one thing is said, often in all sincerity, and we the audience know something very different to be the case).

Is Banquo, however, speaking in all sincerity. Is *'worthy'* something he knows Macbeth has been in the past but merely hopes he will be from now on? It would have been interesting to hear an aside from Banquo about now…

Maybe *'we stay upon your leisure'* has a touch of friendly jest about it – Banquo has earlier commented to Ross and Angus on Macbeth's preoccuption *(line 142)* in what could have been a light-hearted manner.

148

His comment does at least make Macbeth aware of how ill-mannered he has been (or how suspicious his behaviour may have seemed) and he hastens to apologise. He was worrying, he says, about *'Things forgotten'*; but that can hardly mean, as some editors suggest, that he has already forgotten what they were and is therefore lying (and revealing his basic dishonesty). We don't forget things we have been worrying about (*'wrought'*, *line 149*, is quite a strong word) a few moments before. It's more likely that he means 'things I have now laid aside (*deliberately* forgotten) because I need to give you my full attention.' His very formal thanks to them which follow reinforce this impression that he sees how important it is to behave as normally as possible.

149

150-152

[TO BANQUO]: Is Macbeth preparing to seek counsel from a friend or insight into a possible rival's mind?

153-155

He calls them all his friends as they leave. Macbeth's progressive isolation is one of the principal movements of the play.

Overview: other things to note

Setting

o   This encounter takes places on a *'blasted heath' (line 77, and in the stage directions of some editions)*. What dramatic impact does that have?

('Dramatic impact' is a favourite examiner's term. The question can mean various things, such as
- 'What effect does that have on the audience, in the theatre?'
- 'How does that help the dramatist tell his story?'
- 'How does that fact add to our understanding of the play, its ideas or its characters?'

and so on. Examiners shouldn't use it without defining it, perhaps; but unless they do that you can decide for yourself what they mean and answer accordingly. Take your pick, here.)

> o   We have the impression that this place has been destroyed, either by the Witches' lightning or by the battle which has just been fought. Either way, its desolation is appropriate to the mood of the scene.
>
> o   The bareness of the place gives it an unreal appearance, as if Macbeth and Banquo have arrived in a different world – which in a sense they have.
>
> o   *'Blasted'* can also mean 'cursed'; and remember that according to the First Witch Macbeth is a man *'forbid'* (cursed, as well).

Character

o   Banquo: appears to be the stronger character in this scene, mainly in his response to the Witches. He
- is the first to question them *(line 42)*.
- speaks to them somewhat disrespectfully *(lines 44-46)*.
- suggests they are deceitful in their appearance *(lines 54-55)*.
- says he will not beg anything from them and is not afraid of them *(lines 60-61)*.
- is ready to treat them as mere illusions *(lines 79-80, 84-85)*.
- cautions Macbeth against believing too readily what they have said *(lines 122-126)*.
- suspects that Macbeth has been entranced by their pronouncements *(line 142)*.

He also
- is close to Macbeth (*'My noble partner'*, *line 54*) and excuses him to Ross and Angus, who must think Macbeth's behaviour strange.
- is very ready to listen to Macbeth's thoughts about what has happened *(line 155)*.

o   Macbeth: we are given a picture of a man moving simultaneously in opposite directions – hierarchically upwards and morally downwards. The theme of balance again: things equal out.

o   The Witches: they are there by implication (and often by reference) throughout the scene, even after they have left the stage.

o   Inner conflict: we looked earlier (page 8) at the idea that conflict is essential to drama. One type of conflict we listed was 'inner conflict'. It could be argued that the struggles which take place within its characters lie at the heart of *Macbeth* and give it much of its intense power. Maybe Banquo is struggling within himself between *lines 127* and *146*, trying to decide whether to share with Ross and Angus his concerns over Macbeth, and even the details of what the Witches have told them. Macbeth himself certainly struggles in *lines 126-142* to make sense of what he has heard. There are several oppositions in the speech, between the following:

- The truths the Witches have spoken and the uncertainty of what they have promised beyond that
- Macbeth's excitement at the thought of being king and his horror when he begins to imagine what it might take to win the throne
- The constancy of his *'seated'* heart and the fact that it is beating wildly as he thinks about what may lie ahead
- What we are afraid of now *('present fears')* and what we imagine the future could hold *('horrible imaginings')*
- The strength of his body and the fact that it is so easily 'shaken' by his thoughts. (*'Single'* is given by some editors to mean 'weak', but the alternative, 'whole, complete' makes more sense. Macbeth's body is anything but weak.)
- Action *('function')* and thought *('surmise')*
- Present reality (what *'is'*) and future possibility *('what is not')* – the real world and the world of the imagination

Action
o   The idea that the Witches' charm is *'wound up' (line 370)*. That's such a significant phrase within the theory of tragedy. Here are extracts from a speech in Jean Anouilh's *Antigone*:

> *'The spring is wound up tight. It will uncoil of itself…The rest is automatic. You don't need to lift a finger. The machine is in perfect order, it has been oiled ever since time began, and it runs without friction. Death, treason and sorrow are on the march; and they move in the wake of storm, of tears, of stillness…'*

Anouilh argues in fact that it takes only a minor, almost accidental, event to start the spring uncoiling; and the murder of Duncan is certainly neither minor nor accidental. But the idea of things being in place ready to unfold (a similar term) is central to *Macbeth*; and the way they unfold is 'natural', even though they do so within a supernatural framework. It's natural in that it arises from 'the way things are' and follows 'the patterns of existence' we've talked about earlier.

It's also inevitable – much the same thing. Naturalness and inevitability are key concepts in tragedy. Exam questions often focus on them:

That particular question raises a further one – could Macbeth have escaped his fate? We need to be much further into the play before we can consider that.

Style
o   The two different kinds of formality in the scene's dialogue: the supernatural ritualism of the Witches' speech, and the social ritualism of the greetings, apologies and thank-yous which pass among the soldiers

Ideas
o   Illusion *('The earth hath bubbles, as the water has, /And these are of them', lines 79-80)*
o   The idea *(lines 84-85)* that the reason can be taken prisoner ('seized'?) by a herbal potion – the kind of thing which can be prepared and administered by witches. Banquo is right in ways he does not understand.
o   Layers of existence: there is a physical world and a spiritual one. Success in the first depends on support in the other, whether it is support from supernatural forces, your own moral strength, your friends or your wife. If you relinquish your principles and alienate or kill your friends, if your wife deserts you and your supernatural sponsors turn out to have deceived you, then you are doomed. That too is the way things work.

General
o   Structurally this has been a scene of two halves, with much of what is said in the first half giving extra meaning to what is said in the second. That is typical of the pattern of the whole play, in fact, and it demonstrates once more why the 'context' provided by the Witches is so important.

'I think Macbeth "starts" in *line* 51 because he has been secretly thinking about becoming king, and is afraid the Witches – or even Banquo – have read his mind.'

'You mean he was thinking about it even before this meeting?'

'Yes.'

'What's your evidence?'

'Er…'

But it's a reasonable reading of Macbeth's behaviour.

*****

The class want to go back to the question of happiness. How can Banquo be less happy than Macbeth *and* happier?

'It all depends what you mean by happiness' – the answer isn't long in coming, and we go on to discuss it.

Macbeth gets more, so is happier in that sense; but Banquo wants less, so is also happy (i.e. contented…or he would have been if Macbeth had allowed him to live). For a bit of light relief I draw the 'Hagar the Horrible' cartoon on the whiteboard, with Hagar's arm around his son's shoulders as he advises him, 'Son, in this life you have to be content with what you get. So get plenty.' It is Macbeth's attempt, prompted by both the Witches and his wife, to 'get plenty' which in the end ensures that he is left with nothing. Another simple irony.

The concept of greatness (and its opposite) is more relevant to a study of drama, and we talk about that. A tragic hero must be 'great' in some way (at some point in the story, at least), otherwise he doesn't merit our attention. Does he? But what different things can 'great' mean? This is a question the class will have to confront when we study Arthur Miller's *Death of a Salesman*, the tragedy of a man who lies and cheats, bullies and eventually collapses in on himself – one who has no greatness at all, as usually defined, but one to whom, nevertheless (according to Arthur Miller), 'attention must be paid'. For the moment all we have in Macbeth is a hero (central figure) who is a great warrior.

*****

'How come Macbeth doesn't know the Thane of Cawdor has been condemned to death? Look at lines 72-73, when Macbeth asks the Witches, *'But how of Cawdor? The Thane of Cawdor lives, A prosperous gentleman.'* Didn't he fight Cawdor and defeat him? Won't he assume Cawdor is going to be punished, maybe by having his title taken away from him? At least he's not going to be 'prosperous' from now on, is he?'

'But if he was been imagining himself as king earlier, and "started" because he felt guilty when he thought he had been caught doing that, maybe he's trying to cover his tracks in these lines by his questions about Cawdor.'

'You mean by pretending to know less than he does in order to make the idea of becoming king seem ridiculous?'

*****

We return to the matter of stability, which we talked about briefly in the general discussion at the end of the commentary on *Scene One*. Stability is the desired norm in our lives – we want everything to be 'all right' all the time…but things happen to upset that balance:

'Plays are about problems – how they are caused, and how they are solved.'

Relate that statement to your chosen texts.

That shouldn't be too hard to do as far as *Macbeth* is concerned. Macbeth the man has a problem: he wants to be king but is horrified at the thought of what he may have to do to win the throne. All we need to do is show how he solves that initial problem (by screwing his courage to *'the sticking place'* – with his wife's help) then finds that other problems rise beyond the first one, like a mountain range stretching beyond our ability to see. The final solution – well, that's built into the situation itself, from the very beginning (think about the Anouilh quote again).

A simple essay in answer to the question could be little more than a re-telling of the story, with the words 'problem' and 'solution' inserted frequently. The perceptive student, however, will interpret the essay question more widely. It isn't just about the problems faced by the people in a play, it's about all the problems to which the dramatist draws our attention – his problems as someone who sees into the heart of things, our problems, the world's problems, problems of our very existence. We've begun to look at some of those by asking questions like 'How can we know the real truth about anything?' and 'What is happiness, or greatness?' In so doing we're tackling the play's more universal aspects, and coming to an understanding of how a play written so long ago can still be of great interest and value to us today.

*****

Act One Scene Four

Commentary

Duncan shows some slight impatience to know whether or not Cawdor has been executed; but he has to make do with an unofficial report.

1-2

The fact that it *is* unofficial allows it to be anecdotal and therefore more telling. Cawdor's admission of guilt, request for pardon (not relief from punishment, just forgiveness) and repentance are significant. The values of the society against which he rebelled have been reinforced by the manner of his leaving it. He dies in 'becoming' style, and the dignity of his end gives us something against which we can judge Macbeth's behaviour in the face of *his* impending death.

3-11

'Trifle' takes us back to the previous scene. The Witches tempted Macbeth with the trifle of a Thanedom; such things are worth nothing according to Banquo; life itself is a trifle, Cawdor's behaviour at his execution now suggests. So what *does* matter? The *manner* of our living and the *manner* of our dying. Macbeth has a long way to travel before he comes to realise that anything less than a life filled with *'honour, love, obedience, troops of friends'* is *'a tale told by an idiot/Signifying nothing'*.

11

It has been said in some wonderment that *Macbeth* 'is full of quotations.' Here's one you need to remember:

> *'There's no art*
> *To find the mind's construction in the face.'*

11-12

It strikes a keynote in the play. The timing of its delivery is ironic: Macbeth is about to enter. It is possible for an actor playing the lead role to judge his entrance so that he overhears the comment and can visibly react to it.. It would be possible for Macbeth himself, if *he* heard it, to read into it an unsuspecting reference to his own duplicity. A *wise* Macbeth would have read into it a warning about the Witches'.

Note in it, by the way, the image of physical structures – *'construction'* – which Duncan continues in the next line with *'built'*. We found the same point being made in *Scene Two*: what we build (and rely on) in our everyday world must be supported by the realities of the worlds behind that – the moral and spiritual worlds, where people's true minds are to be found.

Is Duncan's speech too gushing? The nicer he is to Macbeth the harder Macbeth will find it to go through with things in *Act Two* and the nastier his actions will seem. So the excessive generosity and warmth of this scene are designed (dramatically) to add to the power of some of the forces with which Macbeth will have to wrestle. (*'He hath honoured me of late'* is one of the reasons Macbeth gives Lady Macbeth for wanting to abandon their plan.)

14-20

Macbeth is cold and formal by comparison. Duncan's speech has been largely in the first person singular and very *personal* (*'My ingratitude...might have been mine...only I have left to say.'*) Macbeth speaks only one *'I'* then switches to *'our (duties)...our (duties)'*, thus distancing himself from this man whom he is now plotting against.

22-27

When he talks about Duncan's *'part' (line 23)*, is he thinking back to the idea of a play in which he is going to steal the leading role? What 'part' is he having to play for the moment?

Now then, pay attention. We're stopping the commentary here so that we can use the rest of the scene as a practice passage at the end of our work on *Act One*. So just read quickly through that section now *(lines 28-58)* – there's some mention of it in the Overview – and be prepared to come back to it later.

Overview: other things to note

<u>Setting</u>
o   This scene establishes more of the context within which Macbeth moves and must lay his plans. What does each of the following suggest about the society to which Macbeth belongs and which is for the moment headed by King Duncan?
- *'Is execution done on Cawdor?' (line 1)*
- *'those in commission' (line 2)*
- *'confessed...pardon...repentance' (lines 5-7)*
- *'The sin of my ingratitude' (line 15)*
- *'our duties /Are, to you your throne and state, children and servants' (lines 24-25)*
- *'We will establish our estate upon /Our eldest, Malcolm' (lines 37-38)*
- *'I'll be myself the harbinger...approach' (lines 45-46)*

- Justice is swift and firm.
- Delegation is the norm ('Why doesn't Duncan fight his own battles?' asked Heather, you may remember).
- The values of society are accepted even by those who have transgressed them.
- Loyalty and courage are to be speedily rewarded.
- There is strict hierarchical structure with the king at the head.
- Stability is something to be preserved.
- Hospitality is valued.

The more ordered and successful this community appears, the greater is Macbeth's crime in attacking it in an attempt to take it for himself.

<u>Character</u>
o   Macbeth and Banquo are not treated equally by Duncan, in spite of his protestations that Banquo has *'no less deserved' (line 30)*. He greets Macbeth first and speaks ten lines to him, only four, or perhaps six, to Banquo. It is at Macbeth's castle that he is going to stay. And it is about Macbeth that he speaks most warmly (to Banquo) at the end of the scene. The relationship between Macbeth and Banquo is very important in the play. Banquo is a moral counterbalance to Macbeth; but he is less important in himself, both to the story and to Duncan.
o   Duncan has been called a weak king. Is that the impression you have of him here? (Question: 'What is 'weak'?' – almost as important as 'What is greatness?' If Duncan *is* weak in any meaningful way, is that being offered by Shakespeare as a reason for Macbeth's actions? Macbeth himself doesn't use it as an excuse, although he does describe Duncan later as having ruled *'meekly' (Act One Scene Seven line 17)*.

<u>Action</u>
o   This is a transition scene: it brings the whole matter of the rebellion to a conclusion (with the death of Cawdor) and prepares the way for the murder at Macbeth's castle – and for, we have noted, the struggle which will go in Macbeth before that murder is committed.

<u>Style</u>
o   The whole scene reminds us how much can be going on beneath the surface of the most formal language. Duncan's immense relief at the fact that he has survived the rebellion, his blind trust, the ready warmth of his relationships, which verges on sickliness – all of these excesses are reflected in the excesses of his words.
o   There's been a leap in the intensity and power of Macbeth's language *(lines 48-53)* as his schemes take shape.

<u>Ideas</u>
o   Appearance and reality: *'There's no art...'* (can you finish the quote?)

o The idea (which barely surfaces) that a weak king deserves to be overthrown (*Richard II* and *Henry IV* are other plays by Shakespeare which, taken together, deal with that issue much more fully)
o The right of the son to succeed his father as king – not discussed in the play, but obviously challenged by Macbeth. It was not an absolute that this should happen in Scotland at that time – which is why the announcement about Duncan's son is such a blow: Macbeth can no longer hope to be given the throne when Duncan eventually dies.
o Justice
o Reward
o Duty

General

o It's been important for us to see more of Duncan, so that we know just who it is Macbeth is killing.

Student Response

'Duncan's a bit naïve.'

Yes he is, we agree. 'Perhaps that's a better word than "weak"'.

'Banquo's a bit naïve as well.'

No he isn't, we decide. He's just reluctant to believe the worst of his friend – and he doesn't set so much store by the Witches' prophecies anyway.

'Isn't Macbeth naïve?' A better question.

*****

'Why so much formality?'

We eventually produce an answer. Formality (working within 'forms', or established structures, whether of language or ceremony or hierarchy) is one way of holding a society together. Scottish society has just been shaken by an almost-successful rebellion. The social formality we see here is one way in which the community is reassuring and strengthening itself again.

'Is binding the same thing as holding together? Duncan says his visit to Macbeth's castle will bind them more closely.'

He does; but this is a different way in which a society is held together, we decide – by its personal, and blood, relationships. Macbeth is about to violate all three types of cohesion – the social (i.e. hierarchical), the personal and the familial.

*****

'I still think Banquo's naïve.'

*****

Act One Scene Five

Commentary

Lady Macbeth is half-way through Macbeth's letter when she enters – a realistic effect.

'By the perfect'st report' ('on the most reliable grounds'): Macbeth is still, in spite of Banquo's   *1-2*
warning, pinning his faith in the *'trifle'* the Witches have given him, as proof that their promises can be
trusted.

*'**Burned** in desire'*: can you recall the word Banquo used to suggest how Macbeth might be excited at   *3*
the prospect of kingship?

> *'That, trusted home, might **enkindle** you to the crown'* (Act One Scene Three lines 120-121)

'Made themselves air': Banquo's *'bubbles'*. They vanished into another world.   *4*

'Rapt': that interesting word again, but this time without any suggestion that he is hiding something –   *5*
he is just 'enraptured'.

'The coming-on of time': Macbeth still hopes that kingship will 'come on' to him without his having to   *7*
do very much. He continues to be reluctant to take any initiative himself – which may be why he is
eager to involve his wife as quickly as possible. She, he knows, has it in her to be pro-active, if that is
what will be needed. Lady Macbeth in her response to this letter shows that she knows her husband
well; there's no reason to suppose that Macbeth knows any less about *her*. So when he says he has
written to her so that she can share the good news, he really means, 'Tell me what to do.'   *8-11*

'Lay it to thy heart' means both 'think it over carefully' and 'keep it to yourself.' Probably nine out of   *11*
ten Lady Macbeths will stick the letter down the front of their dresses when the Messengers enter.
(What will the tenth one do with it?)

The letter is in prose (usual) and Lady Macbeth's response to it is in blank verse (expected). What
effect does the switch from one to the other have?

> o   Macbeth has written in a clear and ordered manner and has kept his excitement in check. His
>   language is largely non-figurative (literal).
> o   Lady Macbeth's speech is strong in both rhythms and imagery. She is immediately more
>   passionate about the prospect before them than Macbeth has so far been.

'What thou art promised': the possibility is so enormous that she cannot speak of it in plain terms – the
prize, and the means to it, are unnameable. All the way through this speech she uses indirect phrases to
refer both to the kingship and to the murder which will lead to it. List them.

> The kingship:
> o   *'be great'*
> o   *'ambition'*
> o   *'what thou wouldst highly'*

Lady Macbeth fears Macbeth's *'nature'*, she says. But she doesn't simply mean that he's too weak for the job. It is his *human* nature which is at fault. That's what *'human kindness'* is – it would be more clearly written as 'humankind-ness', and refers to what makes us people, as distinct from animals – or witches. So Lady Macbeth isn't complaining about Macbeth, but about *us. We* are not fitted for the kind of action which is necessary to make us 'great'; we don't *deserve* greatness.

That essentially human nature (which Lady Macbeth *does* see as weak) is passed down to us through the generations, in the very *'milk'* with which we are nursed. To become truly great we must be prepared to deny our inheritance and act ruthlessly in our own self-interest. So Lady Macbeth's speech is a rejection of all that we have seen happening (in the previous scene) in Duncan's court, where humane (another spelling of the word with slightly different connotations) and kind (in the more modern sense) behaviour is both ordained and practised. Lady Macbeth, in other words, wants Mankind to take a different path in his evolution.

Womankind, too. Women can out-man men. She herself asks in a moment *(lines 45-46)* to have her milk turned to gall (bitter fluid); and in *Scene Seven (lines 54-58)* she claims (boasts, even) that she would snatch her nipple from her feeding baby's mouth and dash its brains out, if she had sworn to do it. You can't get much more of a denial of humankind-ness than that.

It is important that you grasp that full meaning of those easily misunderstood lines *(14-15)*. If you say, in an essay or a commentary, 'Lady Macbeth thinks Macbeth is too kind to kill Duncan,' you'll have missed an opportunity.

Macbeth has been 'seized' by the idea of kingship, you will remember. He in his turn must seize – *'catch'* – the swiftest means to achieve it. Lady Macbeth does not think he will.

The next few line are maybe overburdened with antithesis. It's as if Lady Macbeth has drawn up two lists: A) What Macbeth wants and B) Why he will never get it without help.

She moves from one to the other in a manner which makes for a very contrived speech (and a demanding one for an actress); but the rhythms generated are powerful and convincing. She seems to know what she is talking about.

'Hie thee hither' has some dramatic impact (get used to that phrase). Things are about to move swiftly. Duncan will arrive before night and be dead before morning.

She wants Macbeth here so that she can *'pour [her] spirits'* in his ear. She may mean 'the spirit of boldness (*'valour'*) which will put the new Mankind wholly in control of his own future'. But if you know *Othello* and *Hamlet* you'll perhaps remember that the only thing poured into people's ears in those plays is poison.

'Do seem to have thee crowned withal': the phrasing is strange. (*'Withal'* just means 'with'.) The tense of the verb suggests that Macbeth is already crowned – in the world from which the Witches come, and

14

15

16

16-23

23

24
25

perhaps also in Lady Macbeth's imagination.

'Thou'rt mad to say it': she starts in much the same way Macbeth did earlier; she too has been caught thinking bad things. The unexpected arrival of the king has something of the same impact, briefly, as the knocking on the gate which will wake the household (in *Act Two*) to the discovery of his death. Her reaction here is that of a guilty person. (Some commentators have even suggested that when the Messenger says, *'The king comes here tonight'* she is so far forward in her imaginings that she thinks he means King Macbeth, and is momentarily flustered – *and* guilty – when she comes to her senses.) *29*

She does attack the messenger, rather.

He is apologetic. You probably wouldn't want to contradict Lady Macbeth either. *32*

The messenger has brought *'great news'* ('news of greatness' would be more accurate) and deserves to be rewarded, at least by being taken care of *(line 34)*. *36*

Ravens croak to announce imminent death (it was believed); the more important the death the louder the croak (we might imagine). This one has croaked himself almost to silence. Shakespeare needs us to be aware of just how momentous the impending murder will be: it will shake the very structures of the world.

'Under my battlements': why *'under'*? Why *'my'*? *38*

> o   The impression given is that the battlements will loom over Duncan threateningly. (Look at what he himself says about the castle when he arrives, however.)
> o   This is Lady Macbeth's, not Macbeth's, castle – a telling slip. It will in a sense be her plot too, since she becomes the force which drives it to its conclusion – and she's the one who cleans up afterwards.

Just who or what the *'spirits'* are to which Lady Macbeth refers here and in *line 46* (*'murdering ministers'* – if both sets of supernatural creatures are the same) we don't really, as commentators, know. But as an audience in the theatre we will assume she means the Witches (or something very like). As often in drama it's the impression that matters rather than the facts. *38*

'Unsex me here' doesn't really confuse the issue of the New Mankind discussed above. The New Person will be sexless, and will have neither the softness of a woman nor the principles of a man; there will be no room inside this creature for anything but *'direst cruelty'*. Its blood will be too thick to carry feelings such as compassion (*'remorse'*) to its heart and it will have no conscience (*'compunctious visitings of nature'*). Its intentions will be *'fell'* ('fierce, savage'); and it will be ruthless in carrying them out (nothing will come between its *'purpose'* and the *'effect'*). *39*

Is that purpose, in the end, survival rather than just greatness? If so is it the survival of the individual or of the species? Is Lady Macbeth saying something about what we will need become in order to survive as humans – less human? At the very least she is talking about a blurring of the gender line…

'Nature's mischief' may give us a bit of trouble, unless we see it as referring not to human nature (in which there is not *enough* mischief according to Lady M) but to Nature as a whole (i.e. Creation), including that part of it in which evil spirits live. There are other glosses (possible interpretations), but that's the most straightforward one. *48*

The last part of this speech echoes Macbeth's in the previous scene, where he too calls for the stars to *48-52* hide their fires so that he can act unseen. But Lady Macbeth's thinking and her poetry are much more fully developed.

Night is to be *'thick'* like the blood of the creature Lady Macbeth wishes to become, and will hinder sight in the same way that the thickness of her blood will *'stop up th'access' (line 42)* to human feeling. The darkness (gloomy smoke from hell) in which it will wrap itself will act as a *'pall'* (both a cloak capable of hiding something and a funeral winding-cloth).

'My keen knife': does Lady Macbeth think she will have to commit the murder herself? She almost has to when the time comes.

There are perhaps forces in Creation which could work against the powers of darkness; but they have not been mentioned hitherto, and *'heaven'* receives here only a feeble recognition. The Witches, it seems, will have everything their own way.

Just as Lady Macbeth reckons she can out-man men in ruthlessness, so she now out-does both the Witches and Ross in greeting Macbeth with his new titles.   *53*

Note, however, that she does not yet address him as king.

She has been carried away *('transported')* – into an unreal world, we might suggest – by the news in   *54*
his letter. It is the world of *'hereafter' (line 53)* which exists *'beyond this ignorant present'* and lies in
'the future'. But if things here and now can disappear into thin air (as those *'bubbles'* the Witches did)   *55-56*
how much more likely it is that things offered for some future time will fail to materialise at all, and
turn out to be illusions promised by illusions? We know that; but the two schemers do not, or do not
want to.

(Macbeth does become king, of course, so in that sense the Witches keep their word. His assumption has been that kingship will last, however, and will bring content. That mistake is his, not theirs.)

Macbeth barely greets his wife. He is too full of the news of Duncan's arrival.   *56-57*

The next exchange is full of innuendo (hint and double meaning) – none of it particularly original, but chilling nonetheless. Are they concerned that someone may be listening? Or just afraid to hear themselves utter the terrible words which are in their minds?

Actors have a bit of a problem – it's easy to melodramatise (exaggerate the villainy of) these lines.

'And when goes hence?': 'Go hence' can mean 'depart this life'; in even plainer words…   *58*

> die.

'Tomorrow, as he purposes': how long should an actor pause between *'tomorrow'* and *'as'*?

> Try it for yourself. The longer your pause the more significant will be your qualification of
> *'Tomorrow'*, the more *'as he purposes'* will sound like 'at least that's his plan, but we…'

Lady Macbeth is less ambiguous (*'O! Never /Shall sun that morrow see'*), but she is diverted: she   *58-60*
notices the look on Macbeth's face. What do you imagine that look might be?

> Fear? Guilt? Or shock at how much further down that road she is than he?

'Strange matters. To…': if your edition has a comma after *'matters'*, pretend it's a full stop. That's the only sensible way to punctuate his wife's these lines.   *61*

'Look like the time' means a bit more than just 'behave normally'. Think back to the previous scene. In order to *'look like the time'* at Duncan's court Macbeth had to go along with its jollity and excessive warmth, although he was far from being in the mood for it. *'The time'* means almost 'the fashion' – what is acceptable in the present circumstances. Lady Macbeth is saying, 'Your purpose in behaving in line with the norms of the day will be to *'beguile the time'* (deceive the people around you) so that, like a serpent beneath a flower (a snake in the grass) you will be able to strike suddenly and secretly.' This advice has something in common with the *'spirits' (line 24)* Lady Macbeth wanted so badly to pour into Macbeth's ear; and it does indeed have some poison in it.

'He that's coming': she cannot even name Duncan. There's almost a kind of superstition in this refusal,   *64* as if to name him will be to break a spell. (Compare this with the theatrical tradition that *Macbeth* should be referred to only as *The Scottish Play,* and never by name, or bad luck will befall the production.)

She becomes ambiguous herself. Here are three examples. Try to give two explanations for each.
o *'provided for'*   *65*
o *'great business'*   *66*
o *'my despatch'*   *66*

> o   looked after properly; taken care of (i.e. killed)
> o   important visit by Duncan; wonderful opportunity to kill Duncan
> o   my care, so that he is made welcome; my care, so that he is 'despatched' (murdered)

You may find this word-play a bit heavy-handed. An Elizabethan audience will have loved it.

'All our nights and days to come' has an ominous ring to it simply because it has an optimistic one.   *67* That's the case even if we don't already know that Macbeth will talk poignantly of *'all our yesterdays'* just before he dies.

'We will speak further': this sounds like a man who is looking for a means of delay.   *69*

'Only look up clear': has he been looking physically *down*?   *69*

Lady Macbeth reassures him that all he needs to do is appear calm and she will do everything else. In   *70-71* this she is misleading him just as surely as the Witches…unless she does intend, at this point, to kill Duncan herself?

Overview: other things to note

<u>Setting</u>
o   Lady Macbeth sees and addresses spirits *'Wherever…you wait' (lines 47-48)*; they are in an invisible world outside the one in which she walks up and down reading her husband's letter.

Character
- o Macbeth: our knowledge of him deepens suddenly in this scene. Lady Macbeth's almost scornful account of his character has the effect of bringing him closer to us. He is human (that's her complaint against him). He is human (that is what connects him to us).
- o Lady Macbeth: a wholly startling woman. An encounter between her and the Witches would have been something to behold. (Why do you think Shakespeare did not include such a scene?)

Action
- o This is two scenes run together and divided by Macbeth's entrance. They are telescoped to give the impression of time moving swiftly on.
- o The speed of events (same idea): Lady Macbeth wants Macbeth to *'Hie'* to her; *'the king comes here tonight'* is a sudden and unexpected piece of news; *'our thane is coming'* is the next piece; Lady Macbeth then *'feels the future in the instant'*.
- o Indirect reporting. Several important episodes in the play do not happen on stage but are described by someone who saw them or knows about them. Look out for them and try to analyse the effect produced in each case.
- o Foreboding: the raven, yes; but also the rate of Lady Macbeth and Macbeth's downwards moral slide

Style
- o Its contrasts
- o Its gathering pace as it moves from the ordered letter at the beginning, through Lady Macbeth's intense analyses and invocations to the fragmented dialogue at the end as Duncan's arrival approaches

Ideas
- o Unnaturalness. Our whole discussion of human nature (page 22 above) had to do with that theme, and so does much of what Lady Macbeth says in the scene.
- o Sexuality (manhood as compared with womanhood)

General
- o Macbeth came to his wife looking for advice; by the end of the scene he must feel he has jumped on the back of a wild horse which has galloped away with him. How well *did* he know her?

Student Response

'When Macbeth was in such a hurry to get to his castle and talk to his wife, why did he take the time to write a long letter before he set off?'

There's a dramatic reason: Macbeth's letter allows Lady Macbeth to move ahead of him in her imagination. Part of the tension of the scene rests in her struggle to draw him after her, once they are together. But there should also be, to support our theory about characters' actions needing to be convincing within the context of the play, an internal reason – internal to the story or to Macbeth himself. We look for such a reason.

'He might have thought he was going to be delayed on his journey. He certainly didn't travel at top speed: the messenger who left after him with the news that Duncan was on his way overtook him.'

'He sent the letter express mail.'

'He wants her to know about the prophecy as soon as possible.'

'That's true, but it doesn't answer Carrie's question.'

'Isn't he on his way to Forres to meet with King Duncan? He probably couldn't just take off for home instead.' (The simple answer.)

*****

'This whole thing about human nature and a new kind of person: was Shakespeare really serious about that?'

It would be easy to be pompous and say something like, 'Shakespeare was serious about everything, even when he was making his audience laugh.' An essay might provide a better answer:

> *'Plays take us into worlds different from our own, but must have something to say about issues of importance in the world to which we, the audience, will return.'*

> *Show how issues relevant to today's world have been raised in plays you have studied.*

'What's more relevant than the question of who and what we are, and where we're going?'

That comes out as a bit pompous anyway, but it gives us plenty to talk about. As we go through the rest of the play we can examine each major idea we come across to see whether it's 'an issue of importance in the world to which we, the audience, will return'.

We start, however, with a discussion of just how different Macbeth's world *is* from ours. Not so very, we decide.

*****

'Macbeth might have been happy there if it hadn't been for…?'

'Ambition – 'his tragic flaw.'

'The Witches – the way they tempt him.'

'His wife.'

'Duncan's wetness. Macbeth thinks he would make a better king.'

*****

Act One Scene Six

Commentary

Both Duncan and Banquo mis-read the castle: they fail to perceive its *'mind's construction'* (*Scene Four* – what it's really like, and what's going on inside it) in its *'face'* (outward appearance). The air smells sweet; but inside swirls the *'filthy air'* (*Scene One*) of the plot.

'Gentle senses' reinforces the picture we have had of Duncan.	*3*

Lady Macbeth promised a raven to announce the imminent death of the king; Banquo sees only house-martins (*'martlets'*), a sign that a building is favoured. She suggested her battlements would threaten Duncan; Banquo, listing the features of the castle, finds nothing amiss.   *4*   *6-7*

Don't spend too much time on the next two speeches, nor indeed on the ones after that. Commentators have had considerable difficulty making sense of some of them. That's because they are elaborate 'courtesies' designed not to say anything meaningful but to reassure everyone that the social game is being played properly. Yes, we can read extra meaning into words like *'honoured'* and *'trouble'* and pay some attention to Lady Macbeth's mathematical terminology *('twice...double...single')* and link it to similar references elsewhere in the play; but when all's said and done (and that doesn't take very long) this has been no more than brief but necessary scene noting the arrival of Duncan.   *10,11,14*

If you do want to consider some of the other items which have interested commentators, look at the following.
- o *'purveyor'*: someone who has the job of 'providing for' (remember Lady Macbeth's ambiguous use of that phrase?) an important person.   *22*
- o *'his great love, sharp as his spur'*: his ambition is even sharper, and capable of harm.   *23*
- o *'fair and noble'*: (weakish) irony.   *24*

Overview: other things to note

<u>Setting</u>
- o It's probably dusk. Most of the play's scenes take place at night, or in gloom.

<u>Character</u>
- o Duncan: mild, and florid in speech, as hitherto
- o Banquo: naïve still? He is a man who watches, however: he has drawn his own conclusions about the behaviour of martlets *(lines 9-10)*.
- o Lady Macbeth: she out-courtesies Duncan just as she has out-done everybody else she has dealt with so far.

<u>Action</u>
- o None to speak of.

<u>Style</u>
- o Already dealt with. 'Convoluted' is a useful word.

<u>Ideas</u>
- o Appearance and reality

<u>General</u>
- o If this is what it takes to be a part of Duncan's court, maybe we should think again about seeing that as an example of an ideal society. The apparent emptiness of the speeches – not just Lady Macbeth's – betokens a kind of deceitfulness all its own. Is it *time* for a change in the order of things?

Student Response

'Let's read the next scene.'

*****

Act One Scene Seven

Commentary

Macbeth's opening speech is tricky to read aloud (have a go!) You'll find you need to read it slowly. What will that suggest (to the audience) about what Macbeth is doing?

> That he's struggling with this whole situation, having difficulty both in thinking it through and in expressing his thoughts about it

That's why he says the same thing three times, in different ways, in the first seven lines: he's hoping that one of the ways will lead him beyond the thought that killing Duncan won't be the end of the matter.

'Trammel up...catch': catching is important in the play. Macbeth has been caught by the Witches (seized by the notions they put in his head); Lady Macbeth fears he will not *'catch'* the nearest way to kingship; now he is faced with the impossibility of catching (to *'trammel'* is to catch in a net) the consequences of the murder before they catch up with him.   *3*

'Surcease success': it's partly the word-play which makes this passage awkward to read. *'Surcease'* is the murder of Duncan, *'success'* is what will follow (succeed) from that. Your edition has probably explained that for you. We've noted already what the dramatic impact of this awkwardness is; and here's a thought: the shape of words and their connections is another of the 'patterns of existence' which dramatists make plain to us...There will have been *fun* in this speech for Shakespeare's audience.   *4*

'This blow': Macbeth is already rehearsing the murder in his imagination, and thinking beyond it. He seems to be saying, 'If only such a blow would be the end of the matter *'Here /But here'* (in this present life – *'on this bank and shoal of time'*), then we would risk (*'jump'*) what might happen to us in the after-life, or even *'jump'* (forego) the after-life altogether. But to behave like that is to create a precedent and make it likely that we will suffer in similar fashion.' The proverb 'He who lives by the sword dies by the sword' is a crude equivalent.   *4-9*

It's notable that he generalises his thinking (*'we...our'*) in an attempt to place his dilemma in a wider context as if this is a human dilemma rather than one personal to him; but he then faces up to the particularities of the situation and lays out the *moral* reasons why he should not be contemplating what he is contemplating. (When he says *'double trust'* he could have said 'triple': Shakespeare has missed an opportunity for alliteration.)   *12*

'Bear the knife myself': there has been no discussion of precisely how Duncan might be killed. It's interesting that both Lady Macbeth *(in Scene Five)* and, here, Macbeth imagines that it will be by stabbing (with a knife rather than a sword). Is a knife sneakier than a sword?   *16*

The passage then takes on a religious dimension: killing Duncan would be a sin because he has been a virtuous king.

He has also been a *'meek'* one, however, and although Macbeth may call that a virtue here there's little doubt it will have been a troublesome one in the rough and tumble of Scottish history. (We're back with Heather's early question, 'Why doesn't Duncan fight his own battles?') Certainly Lady Macbeth would have no truck with the idea that the meek should inherit the earth – or be able to bequeath it to their offspring. That's not what her new world order would be about.   *17*

Don't get lost among the confusing images of the next few lines. Pity and the cherubim (a kind of angel), riding the winds of heaven, will work together to ensure the damnation of anyone who kills Duncan. That's all you need to know, really. Really.

21

Macbeth's conclusion to all of the above is that he has no reason to kill Duncan and plenty of reasons why he should not. The only *'spur'* he has to murder him is ambition; and he has come close to admitting in this speech that he has, after all, a *'great love, sharp as his spur'* (Duncan's own phrase, *Act One Scene Six line 23*) driving him in the opposite direction.

25

Riding images have been used to suggest several things – in this speech alone Macbeth's willingness to *'jump'* (over, as on a horse, the life to come); the idea of forces of good galloping against a murderer *(lines 22-23)*; and, now, his fear that his ambition will cause him to fall (either *from* his horse, if we imagine him as leaping so hard into the saddle that he tumbles off the other side; or *with* his horse if he attempts to jump too high an obstacle. Commentators can't make their mind up. Either explanation is fine.)

He has no spur but ambition…and his wife, who now enters (ironical *juxtaposition* if you want a big word or *timing* if you want a simpler one).

Does Macbeth start once more? If so, why?

28

---

o   He has been thinking again about killing Duncan, and feels guilty, or
o   He has been thinking about *not* killing Duncan, and feels guilty.

'What news?': what news does he expect, or hope for – that Duncan has left unexpectedly? Or that Lady Macbeth has decided they should not proceed?

What Lady Macbeth tells him is neither of those. Duncan has almost finished eating. That means he is almost ready to retire. That means it is almost time…

Lady Macbeth challenges her husband. She fears the worst.

29

Macbeth can only answer her first question with a more feeble one of his own.

30

She is brusque again: he should have known better than to leave the dining hall.

30

Her fears are realised. Macbeth's bald statement, legalistic in tone, follows directly on from the end of the speech which his wife's entrance interrupted: it is the conclusion towards which he was moving throughout it. *'This night's great business'* (Lady Macbeth's phrase, *Scene Two line 66*) has become just *'this business'*, and he wants no more of it.

31

Note that he does not use the same arguments to support his position, however. He does not mention betrayal of the *'trust'* Duncan has placed in him as his subject, relative and host. He says nothing about Duncan's virtues as a king. He needs instead reasons which Lady Macbeth will understand, reasons not based on principle or rightness. What he says amounts to, 'We're doing very well as things are – why spoil that?'

Another clothing image. The clothes (of a hero) do fit him, says Macbeth, and they're new and shining, so he wants to enjoy them for a while.

34-5

Count the sentences in Lady Macbeth's next speech. Then see how many of them are questions.

And what questions! What an onslaught!

Question 1: she picks up on his clothing image, disparagingly. She sees him not as a hero but as a | *35*
drunkard who has wrapped himself in a false hope and (Question 2) has fallen asleep in it, and who, | *36*
now he is awake and sober, has no stomach for the enterprise (is green and pale at the thought of it).

Her only statement is even harsher. She dismisses his love for her as just as weak and sickly as his | *38-39*
drunken hope.

Is that an attack on his sexuality? Question 3 seems to embrace both his courage *and* his sexual | *39-41*
performance. It's all very well wanting something, but your performance needs to match your desire.
(Remember this connection she makes when you listen to what the Porter has to say, in *Act Two*, about
drink and lechery.)

Question 4 develops the idea, relating it more precisely to the kingship (*'the ornament of life'* is the | *41-45*
crown). She asks: Is there a wide gap between what he wants and what he is prepared to do to get it?
(Is he like a cat who wants fish but dare not stick his paw in the water?)

This final question is longer and more elaborate than the others; it is the climax of her savage speech.
Its rhythms are powerful (read the whole speech aloud and you'll see). It includes an accusation of
cowardice, and a belittling comparison with a timid animal. No wonder Macbeth protests – *'Pr'ythee,* | *45*
peace.' But how does he speak? There's no exclamation mark. It's a tame response. So is the claim
with which he follows it: If he did any more, he says (is he thinking a military, political or sexual
'more'?), he would be superhuman.

No, says Lady Macbeth, he is less than human (remember her view of what 'human' should mean). He | *47*
is a cat in his cowardice and was a *'beast'* when he shared his plans with her (when was that, by the
way? Nobody seems to know). From *'thou'* he has become the more formal *'you'*. She is punishing
him by moving away from him.

Then there's more about what it takes to be a man. It takes the intention to do great things (which is | *49*
what he had when he *'durst'* begin this whole business); but you have to actually do what you
intend…and the more you do the more of a man you are. (She makes it all sound simple.) She also | *51-52*
says that he showed himself at that earlier point (whenever it was) willing to create opportunity
(*'time…place'*) if none presented itself.

(Not so – not the Macbeth, anyway, who said, *'Let come what come may'* (Scene Three line 146). Is
she mis-representing his earlier behaviour to increase the pressure on him now? Or is there a missing
scene in which he made bolder plans? *Macbeth* is the shortest of Shakespeare's plays. Not your
problem!)

There is play in the next few lines on *'make…made…unmake'*. Macbeth's failure either to create the | *52-54*
opportunities he promised or to take advantage of the ones that have 'made' themselves means that he
has forfeited the right to call himself a man, since according to Lady Macbeth your manhood is
measured by what you do. He is 'unmade' by that failure.

Her horrific boast (it is that) that she could kill her own infant simply in order to do what she has said | *54-59*
she will do is an extension of the same line of argument. The baby she has created is something she has
'done' – willed, and brought, into existence. But she has the power to undo it, unmake it, and would

exercise that power if need be.

Note how graphic her language is, with its physical detail and the sudden verbs *'plucked'* and *'dashed'*.

Her final word is *'this'*. It brings Macbeth back to *'this...great business'* in hand and *'this blow'*. There is no escape for him.

'If we should fail' indicates that he will at least try. But it's a faint commitment still.   *59*

How does your edition punctuate *'We fail'*?
o   *'We fail?'*
o   *'We fail!'*
o   *'We fail.'*

All three ways have been used. What difference does it make? (Imagine yourself reading the phrase aloud.)

Lady Macbeth has him, and she makes sure of him by moving into practical details and thus distracting   *60*
him from any further consideration of right and wrong. Tighten up your courage like a lute string or the
string of a crossbow, she says, to the point where the peg or screw is locked in position and the
instrument is ready for playing (in tune) or the weapon for firing. But it's hard, in *'sticking place'*, not
to think forward to daggers and blood.

Look at the increased warmth of her address, now he is a 'man' again. *'We'll not fail'* – how could   *61*
they, as a team, fail? *'What cannot you and I perform?'* *(line 69)*. The New Man and the New Woman
can do anything.

She ends with two more of her unanswerable questions.   *69-72*

What do Macbeth's next three lines express?
o   Admiration?
o   Disgust?
o   Resignation?

There are no clues. Read the lines so that you convey each feeling in turn, and see which reading
rings truest.

Whatever his feelings there is nothing for it now but to get on with the practicalities. He even offers a   *74-79*
suggestion of his own . Lady Macbeth builds on it. They do, after all work well together.

He is *'settled'*, he says (convinced? or just determined?) He makes it easier for himself by   *80*
concentrating on the physical details of the plan – he will prepare his whole body *('Each corporal
agent')* for what it has to do. *'Bend up'* *(line 80)* perhaps refers back to the crossbow image.

But it remains a *'terrible feat'* that he has committed himself to. And he does at last acknowledge that   *82-83*
he is evil and false. That is perhaps Lady Macbeth's greatest achievement in the scene.

Overview: other things to note

Setting
o   Night
o   This is 'A room in the castle': we have moved deeper into the heart of Macbeth's and Lady Macbeth's dark thinking.
o   Macbeth has won the good opinion of *'all sorts of people' (line 33)*: we have the impression once more that this is a layered but cohesive society.
o   The chamberlains will off their guard, Lady Macbeth believes. This seems such a safe place.

Character
o   Lady Macbeth: such a mixture of passion and practicality, cruelty and warmth, womanliness (yes: her account of how she would kill her baby would be meaningless if the child were not dear to her) and manliness. No wonder she has Macbeth in a spin.
o   Macbeth: in a spin. He comes out of this scene facing in a very different direction.
o   Duncan: an old man (he'll be tired after his journey and fall asleep easily).
o   The chamberlains: expendable

Action
o   The struggle that takes place here is in some ways greater than the one that goes on inside Macbeth before he goes, finally, to Duncan's sleeping chamber. It is between a husband and wife who have a close past and must now decide together what kind of future they want; and it's between two different ways of looking at the world. Conflict indeed.

Style
o   You *could* list the persuasive techniques Lady Macbeth employs. Or you could just pick out a couple of images and show how they work.

Ideas
o   Reputation: Macbeth does not want to jeopardise the *'Golden opinions' (line 33)* he has won; but his reputation has not been easily come by (the word used isn't in fact 'won' but *'bought'*: he has paid dearly for it by the risks he has taken on the King's behalf).
o   Patterns of existence: *'We still have judgement here', line 8* ('we constantly see in this world') that things operate in a particular way; in this case that evil deeds return to harm their perpetrator.
o   Appearance and reality (in the rhyming couplet which rounds off the scene)

General
o   Imagine Macbeth and Lady Macbeth back in the dining hall with Duncan. Try writing part of the scene and maybe even acting it out in class. Use modern English. What you'll probably find is that there's no way of following the scene we've just looked at; and there wouldn't have been even if you were Shakespeare.

Student Response

'Is the first speech what's called a soliloquy?'

Somebody explains that it is: Macbeth is alone on the stage when he speaks (we can ignore the servants who have been passing back and forward in the background). It's a dramatic convention.

We make sure we understand what a dramatic convention is (something which is unrealistic but acceptable in a play in order to make it work as the dramatist wants it to, e.g. characters speaking blank verse; or a cut-out tree representing a whole forest; or masks; or letters used awkwardly to convey important information; or someone, as here, speaking his thoughts out loud).

*****

'What's the point of a soliloquy?'

'It lets you see into a character's mind.'

'Why is it important to see into characters' minds?'

'That's usually the most interesting part of a play.'

'That's how we feel to be a part of what's going on.' A better answer…so an essay:

> *'Unless a dramatist establishes a corridor down which the audience can approach the play, nothing will be communicated, the play will not work.'*
>
> *How far and in what ways in the plays you have studied do the playwrights attempt to bring the audience close to the events taking place on stage?*

Soliloquies are a part of that.

It's not time to tackle that essay question yet, however. There are more soliloquies to read first…and there are other methods of reaching out to an audience. We'll look out for them.

'Is writing about issues of our time one of them?' Good start.

*****

Additional questions (A Level)

A Level questions are often more limited in their focus – directed towards particular aspects of particular plays. Here are some sample *Macbeth* questions, based on the first act only. A Level questions covering the whole play will be given at the end of the guide.

> *1. What indications have we been given by the end of Act One of 'Macbeth' that the action will move towards a tragic conclusion?*
>
> *2. What different kinds of conflict have you noted in the first act of 'Macbeth'?*
>
> *3. What elements in the first act of 'Macbeth' will encourage us to read on – or stay in our theatre seats?*

Commentary Practice - General

Whether you are preparing for an A Level or AP written exam or for the IB Individual Oral Commentary, you will need to practise the techniques of textual analysis: it's not enough to know the play well. AP students particularly will need to know how to take a piece of writing apart if they are to answer the first two Free-Response questions successfully.

IB Literature, IOC (Individual Oral Commentary): Standard Level candidates will be given a passage of up to forty lines and asked to talk about it for ten minutes, after a period of silent preparation. Guiding questions will be attached to the passage to help them focus on some of its important aspects. Higher Level students will be asked to base their Individual Oral Commentary on a poem rather than a piece of fiction or drama; but some of the skills they can acquire by looking in detail at passages from *Macbeth* will be invaluable in their analysis of the work of their chosen poet.

IB Language and Literature, IOC (Individual Oral Commentary): Candidates will be given a passage of up to forty lines and asked to talk about it for fifteen minutes, after a period of silent preparation. Guiding questions will be attached to the passage to help them focus on some of its important aspects.

GCE A Level candidates may be asked to write a commentary on a selected passage or short scene, either with or without guiding questions (which may in any case be as vague as, *'Discuss the dramatic significance of this passage.'*) This part of the exam is sometimes called a 'context question'.

You won't ready yet for a test like that if you're reading the play for the first time: you will need to know the whole play so that you can say something about how the passage fits into it (what the passage's 'context' is, in other words).

So you may for the moment just want to take a quick look at the sample questions and answers on the following pages then come back to them when you've finished the play. It's important before you study the text any further that you realise how much detail you will have to go into in your commentary. Basically you will need to look closely at every word, phrase, line and sentence of the commentary passage to see whether they can help you answer the question or questions.

Here's a passage, then, with guiding questions, from *Act One*. It's the first of five sample passages (one from each act of the play). Taken together, and in order, they are designed to lead you into commentary work by giving you lots of help to begin with then decreasing amounts as you become more expert.

The next few pages include:

o   A sample passage from the very end of *Act One Scene Three* (you may not be given the act and scene reference in the actual exam), with guiding questions
o   Some suggestions about how to make notes in answer to the questions
o   An example of the same passage marked (with underlining) as part of the note-making process
o   Sample notes on the passage (referring to the underlined words and phrases)
o   A full commentary on the passage (written as if it's being delivered orally from the notes. It would also be fine as a written commentary, however, with some tidying-up of the informal language).

Sample passage

DUNCAN: Welcome hither:

    I have begun to plant thee, and will labour

    To make thee full of growing. [to BANQUO] – Noble Banquo,

    That hast no less deserved, nor must be known

    No less to have done so, let me infold thee,   *5*

    And hold thee to my heart.

BANQUO: There if I grow,

    The harvest is your own.

DUNCAN: My plenteous joys,

    Wanton in fullness, seek to hide themselves

    In drops of sorrow. – [To ALL] Sons, Kinsmen, thanes,

    And you whose places are the nearest, know,   *10*

    We will establish our estate upon

    Our eldest, Malcolm; whom we name hereafter

    The Prince if Cumberland: which honour must

    Not, unaccompanied, invest him only,

    But signs of nobleness, like stars, shall shine   *15*

    On all deservers. – [To MACBETH] From hence to Inverness,

    And bind us further to you.

MACBETH: The rest is labour, which is not used for you:

    I'll be myself the harbinger, and make joyful

    The hearing of my wife with your approach;   *20*

    So, humbly take my leave.

DUNCAN: My worthy Cawdor!

MACBETH [Aside] The Prince of Cumberland! – That is a step

    On which I must fall down, or else o'erleap,

    For in my way it lies. Stars, hide your fires!

    Let not light see my black and deep desires;   *25*

    The eye wink at the hand, yet let that be,

    Which the eye fears, when it is done, to see.   [Exit]

DUNCAN: True, worthy Banquo, he is full so valiant,

    And in his commendations I am fed;

It is a banquet to me. Let's after him, *30*

Whose care is gone before to bid us welcome:

It is a peerless kinsman.

Guiding questions

a) How are personal and public matters intermingled in this passage?
b) What do we learn from the passage about the relationships among the characters? Pay special attention to the language they use.

How to make notes in answer to the guiding questions

o Read the passage through carefully, paying attention only to the meaning of the words – what is being said and done, and by whom.
o Work out where in the play the passage comes from – what has happened just before it, what happens just after. Jot down that information at the top of the page (either the page on which the passage is written or a separate piece of paper).
o Read the passage again, very carefully, and note, line by line, anything which will help you answer the questions. You may decide to read it once for each question (if there's more than one), making a separate set of notes each time. (IB students whose teachers have been really kind to them may in that case have provided two copies of the passage.)
o Consider using a colour coding system (underlining or highlighting) as you're going through the passage to mark bits you want to comment on. Remember that you will be working under pressure, whether you're taking an oral or a written exam: anything which will help you avoid getting confused and forgetting something important is worth trying.
o Add your own brief notes on what you want to say about each of the underlined items. Do not try to write whole sentences.
o Base your notes on the details of the passage itself, not on what you know in general about the characters and events of the play – unless you have been asked to show how the passage *reflects* what you have learnt elsewhere.
o At the bottom of the page note something really important about the passage (whether or not you've already mentioned it). You will be able to use that as a conclusion to your commentary.
o Have a last look through the passage if there's time, to make sure you haven't missed something obvious.
o Take a deep breath and start.

If any of the above contradicts what your teacher advises you or the examiner tells you to do, go with your teacher or the examiner (except for the bit about taking a deep breath).

On the next two pages you will find a copy of the passage with notes added as suggested.

Sample passage with underlining: <u>Question a)</u> <u>Question b)</u>

DUNCAN: Welcome hither:

    <u>I have begun to plant thee</u>, and <u>will labour</u>

    <u>To make thee full of growing</u>. [to BANQUO] – Noble Banquo,

    That hast no less deserved, nor must be known

    No less to have done so, <u>let me infold thee,</u>   *5*

    <u>And hold thee to my heart</u>.

BANQUO: <u>There if I grow,</u>

    <u>The harvest is your own.</u>

DUNCAN: My plenteous joys,

    Wanton in fullness, seek to hide themselves

    In <u>drops of sorrow</u>. – [To ALL] <u>Sons, Kinsmen, thanes,</u>

    <u>And you whose places are the nearest, know,</u>   *10*

    We will establish our estate upon

    <u>Our eldest, Malcolm</u>; whom we name hereafter

    <u>The Prince if Cumberland</u>: which honour must

    Not, unaccompanied, invest him only,

    But signs of nobleness, like stars, shall shine   *15*

    On all deservers. – [To MACBETH] <u>From hence to Inverness,</u>

    <u>And bind us further to you</u>.

MACBETH: <u>The rest is labour, which is not used for you:</u>

    <u>I'll be myself the harbinger</u>, and <u>make joyful</u>

    <u>The hearing of my wife with your approach;</u>   *20*

    So, humbly take my leave.

DUNCAN: <u>My worthy Cawdor!</u>

MACBETH [Aside] <u>The Prince of Cumberland! – That is a step</u>

    <u>On which I must fall down, or else o'erleap,</u>

    For in my way it lies. <u>Stars, hide your fires!</u>

    <u>Let not light see my black and deep desires;</u>   *25*

    The eye wink at the hand, yet let that be,

    Which the eye fears, when it is done, to see.   [Exit]

DUNCAN: True, worthy Banquo, <u>he is full so valiant,</u>

    <u>And in his commendations I am fed:</u>

    <u>It is a banquet to me. Let's after him,</u>   *30*

    Whose <u>care</u> is gone before to bid us welcome:

    It is a peerless <u>kinsman</u>.

Question a):How are personal and public matters intermingled in this passage?
o   *(2)* Everyone dependent on the king's favour – needs to be '*planted*' by him.
Duncan:
o   *(9)* personally affected – he weeps.
o   *(9)* makes very public announcement.
o   *(10)* includes everyone close to him.
o   *(12-13)* refers informally to son*)* but gives him very public title.
o   *(17)* his visit to M's castle a private one designed to strengthen their ties; but *(19)* M must see that everything is in place – D is the king after all.
o   *(22-23)* the public announcement about his son has very private implications for M.*)*
o   *(28)* M described as '*valiant*'– a public judgement – but also *(32)* a relative.

Question b): What do we learn from the passage about the relationships among the characters? Pay special attention to the language they use.
o   *(2)* D uses informal image (gardening) in thanking Macbeth: feels warmly towards him.
o   *(5-6)* D uses intimate language to B.
o   *(6-7)* B equally warm back and uses same gardening image.
o   *(16)* D jovial towards M *(16)*
o   *(18)* M stiff in response
o   *(19-20)* Hidden meaning in M's words – relationship not what D thinks.
o   *(21)* Even clearer irony
o   *(24-25)* Powerful imagery of deception
o   *(31)* Irony
o   *(29)* D about M –intimate language again

You might be able to fit your notes around and in between the lines of the printed passage, if your handwriting's small and the margins are wide. The advantage of that as far as oral commentary is concerned is that everything will be on the same page and you will be able to draw lines to connect each comment with the quotation which illustrates it. Try to avoid having to flip back and forward between two sheets of paper – you're likely to get lost at some point.

It's usually easier to deliver/write your commentary line by line; but A Level candidates writing a 'free' commentary (i.e. if they are given no guiding quotations, or only a very general one) can still use a colour coding system to organise their commentary under headings like the ones we gave earlier (*Setting, Character, Action* etc).

Model commentary

Some tips:

o   Begin by giving the brief details you noted about where the passage come in the play. Do not tell the whole story as it's happened so far.
o   Use in your commentary the quotations on which you are basing your comments.
o   You can add in new thoughts as you speak or write.
o   Indicate when you are moving from one question to the next.
o   End by making the final important point you included in your notes. This will show the examiner that you can think beyond the guiding questions and could in fact say or write more if you had the time.
o   Try to give the questions roughly equal time (if there's more than one).

Here's the sample. If you're an IB student you could try reading parts of it into a tape recorder (you need to practise speaking into a microphone anyway), just so that you get used to the sound of your own voice saying things like this. (Yes, you may feel a bit silly to start with, but stick with it.)

Note: you'll soon see that we've deliberately chosen a difficult passage – difficult because it's not that interesting in itself, and because at first sight there doesn't seem to be a lot to say in answer to the questions. But if you persevere and look at absolutely every bit of the text – more than once – you'll be surprised how much eventually emerges.

Examiners don't always choose the 'best' extracts for you to write or talk about…

'This passage is taken from *Act One*. Macbeth and Banquo have arrived at the king's palace after the battle (and after they have met the Witches). Duncan thanks them for their victory over the rebels, and at the end of the scene arranges to visit Macbeth's castle in Inverness.

'There is a strong connection between the public and private events in the scene. It takes place at court and there are a number of people present They will be listening carefully to what is going on. It is quite a ceremonious scene, overall.

'Everyone depends on the king: being 'planted' by him means being favoured – you are assured of success. We have the impression of a large and well-ordered society. But some of his relationships are very personal, and he is deeply affected by them. He weeps with gratitude when he thinks about what Macbeth and Duncan have done for him in defeating the rebels.

'The announcement of the fact that his son will be Prince of Cumberland is made formally – he demand's everyone's attention first. But he doesn't just address the people of rank, he includes everybody who is 'near' to him.

'He talks about his son fondly – he calls him 'our eldest' – but he gives him a very important title, indicating that he expects him to be king one day. That public announcement has very private implications for Macbeth.

'We aren't sure why Duncan is going to stay at Macbeth's castle, but he says he is going to take the opportunity to come closer – 'bind' himself – to his 'valiant' kinsman. 'Valiant' emphasises the bravery Macbeth has shown on behalf of the whole community: he is a public hero. But he is a relative as well.

'Macbeth is also aware of the dual position he holds. Even though Duncan is his kinsman, he is also the king and must be very well looked after. So he leaves ahead of the main party to make sure everything is organised properly. (At least that's why he says he's going.)

'The second question asks what we learn from the passage about the relationships among the characters.

'The style of speech the characters use is mixed, just like their relationships.

'Duncan uses an informal image (gardening) when he thanks Macbeth: he obviously feels warmly towards him. His words to Banquo in lines 5 and 6 are also friendly and informal. Banquo is just as warm in his reply, and uses the same gardening image – 'the harvest is your own.'

'After Duncan has made his announcement about his son he turns to Macbeth again and makes plans for his journey: 'From hence to Inverness.' His tone is jovial. Macbeth's reply, however, is stiff and cold – he has been taken aback by the announcement, and maybe even feels that Duncan has let him down.

'He is already hiding things from Duncan. When he says Lady Macbeth will be happy when he tells her about the king's visit, he knows that what she will really be is excited about how that may help the Witches' prophecy come true. So 'make joyful the hearing of my wife with your approach' has a double meaning. (That's typical of the style of several speeches in the play.) The relationship between the two men is not what Duncan thinks it is.

41

'The irony in line 21 is even more obvious. Duncan calls Macbeth 'worthy'. We know that he is not, and that he is plotting against his benefactor.

'Macbeth uses physical imagery to show how he views the fact that Duncan has given his son the title 'Prince of Cumberland' – 'step', 'fall down' 'o'erleap' – it is a physical problem and will have to be dealt with physically. The rhyme in the last four lines emphasises how strongly he feels

'The imagery of deception is even more powerful in lines 24-25. Macbeth wants the stars not to shine so that his wicked plans will remain hidden. He is planning to deceive his king, and his friend Banquo, and the whole community.

'There is more irony in line 31. Duncan thinks Macbeth is travelling to Inverness ahead of them so that he can take care of his king. Yes, he is, but Macbeth means something very different by 'take care' – 'get rid of'. The irony of that is brought home by the intimate and warm way Duncan speaks about Macbeth in the next few lines. It's as if he is nourished by the good things he hears about Macbeth.

'Banquo for his part has clearly been praising Macbeth warmly ('full so valiant'): his friendship for him seems to be undiminished in spite of his suspicions.

'Duncan's eagerness to reach Macbeth's castle to be with him once again is reflected in his informal phrase, 'Let's after him'. There is more irony in that eagerness.'

Not very exciting stuff; but you have to make the best of what you're given. Try to get interested; or at least *sound* as if you're interested. Further tips follow.

Commentary – Further Suggestions

Written Commentary:
o Don't write a rough draft and then copy it up. That's a waste of valuable time.
o If you make mistakes (and you will) don't scribble them out, even if you decide they're stupid and you don't want anybody to see them. Just put a neat line through them. The examiner will ignore them.
o Keep an eye on the clock: try to get through to your final 'important' point(s) so that you have rounded off your commentary.

Oral Commentary:
o Speak slowly and steadily.
o Pause between points.
o Take the time to make sure you're in the right place in your notes. You could tick off each point with a pen when you've made it.
o If you get lost or think you've run out of things to say, the examiner (probably your teacher) will ask you further questions to help you along.
o Don't worry if you don't have time to say everything you planned to. If the examiner has to interrupt you because time's up, that's good (make sure, however, that you've said a fair bit in reply to both questions).
o Don't whatever you do try to write out the whole commentary so that you can read it out loud. That won't work.

Act Two

Act Two Scene One

Commentary

'How goes the night?'   *1*
- o   Surface meaning: 'What time is it?
- o   Deeper meaning?

> 'I wish this night was over.' Banquo is a troubled man.

He and his son have difficulty answering the question even in its superficial form. Time has become   *2-3*
suspended, and will not move again until Macbeth has murdered Duncan. The audience, too, is now in
suspense.

'Hold, take my sword': Banquo is going through the motions of preparing for sleep.   *4*

Macbeth and Lady Macbeth have both had their wish (*'Stars, hide your fires!' Act One Scene Four line*   *4-5*
50, and *'Come, thick night' Act One Scene Five line 48*; but you won't be expected to quote the lines,
and certainly not to give line references: the fact itself will do.)

Banquo needs to sleep but does not want to, because of the dreams that may come. These are *'cursed'*   *8-9*
in that they are about actions that if carried out will bring a curse on the perpetrator. What might his
dreams be about?

> - o   His own ambitions?
> - o   His fear that Macbeth may be plotting something?

It's an important question. We need to decide as we read this scene through just what is in Banquo's
mind when he talks to Macbeth. If he's worried only about the bad (ambitious) thoughts he himself is
having, arising from the Witches' promise that his sons will be kings, then his conversation here is
fairly straightforward and inconsequential. If on the other hand he is concerned about what may be
going on in *Macbeth's* mind, some of the things he says take on a second meaning (and there are lots
of 'second meanings' in the play).

'A friend': note the shortness of the line. The claim hangs in the air.

Banquo calls Macbeth *'Sir'* twice, but that doesn't necessarily mean anything – it may be no more than   *11*
respect between equals. By the same token we shouldn't assume that Macbeth's use of *'we'* and *'our'*
later in the scene means that he is already (unconsciously, even) using the royal plural. Look at each
example as it occurs and decide for yourself – there are usually other explanations.

'Our': Macbeth does speak very stiffly, doesn't he? Is he on his guard, or just on edge?

'All's well': Banquo is just reassuring Macbeth that his hospitality has been up to standard. All is   *18*
clearly not well in the more general sense. That's why he moves suddenly into his question about the
Witches. Is he
- o   wanting to unburden himself to Macbeth about his own thoughts?   *19*

o   trying to find out what's in Macbeth's mind?

> It all depends, as we said earlier, on how we read his concerns in this whole scene.

He's not going to get very far, in either case. Macbeth defers the discussion; and before it can take place the whole situation, we know and he knows, will have changed enormously.   *22*

'We': ?   *23*

It's Macbeth's turn to sound Banquo out, but he does so very vaguely.   *25-26*

These lines suggest more than any other that Banquo is suspicious of Macbeth. They're a direct   *26-29*
warning to Macbeth that Banquo will not allow himself to be involved in any dirty business. Macbeth,
on the other hand, will *'lose'* honour (merit) by trying to increase his honour in another sense – power
(honours, title). Banquo makes it plain that he believes he is *'franchised'* (owned by the king) to whom
he has a *'clear'* (unqualified) loyalty.

Macbeth has learned only something he did not want to hear, and leaves abruptly.

'Repose' might seem threatening if we read it in the light of what Macbeth does to Banquo later, but   *29*
that's probably looking too far ahead.

'Sir': as above.   *30*

'The like to you': Macbeth will have trouble with repose as well (if you want to look even further
ahead).

Macbeth and his wife have continued to make detailed practical plans – a way of making sure   *31*
Macbeth's scruples don't get in the way again.

They could well do. The dagger appears to him, perhaps, as he hesitates: a director or actor will have a   *34*
choice as so what Macbeth does between the servant's exit and Macbeth's next words. Does he stand?
Walk? For how long?

Once again, as was the case with Banquo's part in the exchange which has just taken place, how we
see the overall passage will determine how we read some of its details. It could be any one of the
following.
o   Simply the hallucination of a mind *('heat-oppressèd brain')* under too much strain
o   A subconscious attempt by Macbeth to escape the situation – he might have gone on to have
    imagined the dagger leading him away from Duncan's bedroom; or he could have imagined it
    pointing towards him, warning him off. But no, the handle, not the point, is *'towards'* his hand,
    and the dagger leads him towards the bedchamber.
o   Shakespeare reminding us that Macbeth is being guided by strange forces which he cannot control

The overall dramatic purpose of the speech is, strangely, rather unclear. But it is powerful enough in
itself not to need a purpose beyond that of gripping the audience at a terrifying moment in the play's
forward movement.

Why does he try to clutch the dagger?

'Fatal vision': this is either because the dagger is going to be fatal to Duncan, or because it is part of   *36*

these 'fatal' events (i.e. events ordained by fate). If the second, then that reinforces the impression we may have that Macbeth is still unwilling to accept responsibility for what he is intending to do. *'Marshall'st' (line 42)* implies some degree of compulsion.

Why does he draw his own dagger at this point?   *41*
o   To compare it with the visionary one?
o   To reassure himself that he is still awake – and in the real world?
o   To defend himself against the forces he feels himself surrounded by?
o   To kill Duncan? (But he still has to get to the bedchamber, and he may meet someone on the way
    – Banquo has barely retired. Has he forgotten, too, that the plan was to use the grooms' own
    daggers? Is this the first of the several mistakes Macbeth makes?)

'The way that I was going': <u>was</u> he delaying? Does this mean, 'I was going, I was going – really I   *42*
was'?)

Just which of his senses is he to believe? He can't decide. Which of the voices speaking to him (the   *43-44*
Witches', Banquo's, Lady Macbeth's, his ambition, his conscience) should he have listened to? 'Who
to trust?' – one of the play's central questions.

The *'gouts of blood'* appear while he is looking at the dagger: this is a developing situation – things   *46*
are happening as he speaks.

'This night's great business', which became briefly *'this business'*, has grown again to a *'bloody*   *47*
business'* which is making him see things that do not exist.

Half the world is in darkness, and evil reigns. It is *his* half of the world, and he accepts with increasing   *49-56*
resignation that he belongs there. In that half of the world Nature (human nature, humankind-ness?)
'seems dead', and only witches and Murder are abroad.

He may be imagining that Duncan is about to become one of the Witches' sacrifices to Hecate; the   *51*
irony of that would be that it is he who is the sacrifice, the offering made (very ritualistically, we will
see in the opening scene of *Act Four*) to the goddess of witchcraft.

There are some confusing pictures in the next few lines. Don't concern yourself too much with   *52-60*
questions like, 'Is a *ravishing stride* something you'd take if you wanted to move stealthily, or you
were old and withered, or a ghost?' and 'Why is Macbeth worried about the stones crying out as he
walks on them and thus spoiling the effect of the silence?' Basically, he's rambling; and it is his
realisation that he's rambling (and delaying again) which causes him to firm up his resolution in the
final lines of the speech.

Why do four of the final five lines rhyme?

To give the *impression* that he's firmed up his resolution. He has gone past being *'settled'* and is
now about to act.

What else coveys his new-found determination?

o   The brief antithesis of *line 60*
o   The proverbial ring of *line 61*
o   The simple certainty, and present tense, of *'I go, and it is done' (line 62)*

> o   The clear sound of the bell
> o   His reference to what will happen to Duncan after he is dead

There's another irony, however. Duncan is quite likely to go to heaven. But Macbeth?

Overview

Setting
o   Still night, of course, and a dark one
o   The world is in two halves, dark and light, good and bad.

Character
o   Macbeth's plain willingness to lie plainly *('I think not of them', line 21)*
o   The contrasts between Macbeth and Banquo, and the tension between them

Action
o   Stories can be told, in part, by symbolic actions. See how Banquo takes off his sword in preparation for sleep, then quickly takes it back again when he hears someone approach. What does he do with it when he realises it is Macbeth who has entered? And what does Macbeth do with the diamond Banquo gives him on behalf of the king? Does he tuck it into a pocket, and is he therefore carrying it, a symbol of Duncan's gratitude, when he kills him?

Style
o   The way Macbeth and Banquo move back and forward between easy informality and a colder style of speech altogether. They are uncertain in their relationship.

Ideas
o   Human nature: Banquo's bad dreams come only when his *'nature /Gives way to'* them, i.e. when he's asleep. Human nature is thus seen as something which must be sustained by awareness and reason; it is also something which can be overwhelmed by sleep, drugs *('the insane root /That takes the reason prisoner'* Act One Scene Two lines 84-85) or drink (the chamberlains' *'natures'* will be *'drenched'* with wine). Or by passion (ambition).
o   Appearance and reality – and illusion (the dagger)…and 'Who to trust?' as noted

General
o   Does Fleance understood anything of what's going on in the first half of the scene? His own future is very much at stake.
o   We have the feeling that Macbeth doesn't understand what's going on in the second half.

Student Response

'Does the dagger Macbeth sees symbolise the murder he is about to commit?'

'What about the dagger he pulls out? Isn't that a more powerful symbol?'

We talk about symbols and what form they can take, including symbols pictured only in words. Crowns are referred to, but it will be up to the play's director whether Duncan actually wears one. The *idea* of a crown is what is important. But what we actually *see* on stage can be more telling.

We list the physical symbols which will have appeared on stage so far – there aren't many.

'Can actions be symbolic?'

Yes, we decide; but it all has to work at a realistic level: there has to be a reason (reasons again) why Banquo takes off his sword and puts it back on again. Macbeth's letter must make sense as a letter. If the thing itself doesn't ring true the idea behind it won't either.

Symbols are also are a way in which the dramatist communicates with the audience, (i.e. they add by visual means to our understanding of what is happening).

> *'In a play the physical objects we see on stage, the actions of the characters, and the words and images they use when speaking must seem real; but they must also, in drama which is to last, mean something beyond themselves.'*

> *Use this statement as a starting-point for a discussion of symbols in plays you have studied.*

Another essay for later. No reason why the class shouldn't make notes on the topic as we go along, however.

*****

Act Two Scene Two

Commentary

Lady Macbeth has drugged the chamberlains with drink; but she herself is under the influence of something else – the excitement of the moment and the thought of what it will lead to: her *'fire'* recalls *'enkindle'* and *'burned in desire'* earlier.   *1*

'Hark! – Peace!': the first sudden exclamation will startle the audience; the second one, Lady Macbeth's attempt to reassure herself, will prepare us for the tension and swings of the scene.   *2*

The owl's cry is the first of a whole series of references to things which happen off-stage – an important effect discussed under Setting below.   *3*

The owl reference echoes the image of the raven which in Lady Macbeth's imagination would welcome Duncan to the castle and to his own death.

'He is about it': the simplicity of the statement, which accepts the plain fact of the matter, is horrific   *4*
enough; but it is added to by the vagueness of its terms: it is assumed that we will know who 'He' and what 'it' are. We are implicated.

'The doors are open': remember what we said about symbolism. What does this image suggest?

'Mock their charge': fail in their duty. Parallels with Macbeth?   *6*

'Do contend...die': one of the struggles and uncertainties of the scene.   *8*

Macbeth's cry (off-stage): consider its dramatic effect. Have things gone wrong? That's what Lady Macbeth thinks. She lacks confidence in Macbeth's ability to do this. (So did he.)

She has carried out all the initial preparation, and came close to committing the murder herself. The   *11*
fact that she could not because Duncan reminded her of her father reminds us that...what?

---

o   Family ties matter.
o   She is not *wholly* inhumane. She would have killed her baby only because she had given her
     word to do so; she has not promised to kill Duncan, but just to help her husband do it.

'The deed': Macbeth still shies away from naming it.   *14*

The fragmentation – jerkiness – of the next part of their exchange conveys their anxiety. Before they   *16-20*
can settle the question of what one sound was, they hear another.

Then Macbeth's attention is caught by the sight of his hands. *'Sorry'*, a very 'human' term, makes   *21*
plain how inhuman the action of his hands has been. Lady Macbeth's response seems harsh, but she is
struggling to remain in control of the situation and her husband. Note the balance of her statement, and
the effect of the alliteration.

It seems to have been Duncan's sons, Malcolm and Donalbain, who half-woke in the room next to   *22*
Duncan's. That adds to the intensity of the moment – their father was being murdered a few yards
away. The picture of Macbeth standing listening to them adds suspense. The laughter of one of them is   *23*
a bizarre extra touch.

Committing a foul act makes it impossible for us to perform some normal ones ever again – pray, and sleep…and trust our friends.

28-32

The only way Lady Macbeth could bring Macbeth this far was by distracting him from thinking – by bullying him, by getting him to focus on practicalities. Now thinking becomes a real danger, to both their security and their future content.
o   *'Consider it not so deeply'*
o   *'These deeds must not be thought'*
o   *'the ravelled sleave of care' (line 36)*

And she includes herself: *'will make us mad'* – prophetic.

When Macbeth talks of sleep he is thinking beyond that. Just as sleep is a kind of cure for the troubles of the day, so our final sleep – life after death – is a reward for the sufferings of our life. Macbeth has debarred himself both from sleep and from heaven – *'great nature's second course'*, the main part of our existence.

38

Such thoughts are beyond Lady Macbeth. Does she lack a 'spiritual' sense?

39

Macbeth ignores her: he is for the moment beyond her reach. He is immersed in the thought that none of his three 'persons' will ever rest again. Because Glamis, the ambitious thane who was delighted to become Cawdor and wanted to be king, has murdered sleep in murdering Duncan, the man beneath the titles – Macbeth – will also suffer.

40

She has to resort to scorn to bring him to what she would call his senses. He is unbending his strength as if he is winding down the crossbow he prepared earlier. He is *'brainsickly'*, another image of paleness, queasiness and cowardice. She challenges him over his mistake with the daggers. (Commentators have worried that she did not seem to notice them earlier, when Macbeth drew attention to his hands; but she must have done. She did not need to use them until now.) **'These daggers'** – does she grasp his hands and hold them up, with the daggers still in them?

45

47

'The place': that vagueness again.

Earlier in the play, imagining was seen as more powerful than actual seeing. Now things have changed: Macbeth will not look on Duncan's body – thinking about it is bad enough. This is another way in which he has been deceived. The reality is, when it comes, more terrible than any picture of it we may have had beforehand.

49-51

Lady Macbeth's answer (apart from the scorn of *'Infirm of purpose'*) is to argue that what is in the bedchamber is only a picture of death, not real. But she contradicts herself when she suggests that Duncan may still be bleeding.

54

You may find the tired pun *'gild…guilt'* well…tired. But puns *were* well-used in Elizabethan drama, and the fact that Lady Macbeth falls back on a worn jest may be another part of her attempt to move things back towards the normal.

55-56

The knocking at the gate: much has been written about it and its theatrical effectiveness. Think about that, in this and the next scene.

'Appals': suggests fear *and* paleness again – the two go together.

57

He has briefly forgotten about his hands. Why do they reach to pluck out his eyes?

> They do not want to be seen, just as he himself did not want to be seen (by the stars) when he committed the murder.

He and his wife have differing views of the scale of things. *'Some water' (line 45)*, *'a little water' (line 66)* will be enough, Lady Macbeth thinks, to wash the blood from their hands. Macbeth doesn't agree…and he makes his point twice, once in elaborate language, once in plain. *59-62*

The practical wife takes over once more. She uses a mixture of scorn (again) and optimism to urge Macbeth along. His resolution has left him, and he is unguarded, she warns him. His thoughts are a danger to him. *63* *70-71*

But his thoughts make him what he is. That is what Macbeth believes. He cannot stop thinking about what he has done. But thinking about what he is done is too painful. So he must stop being what he is (a thinking man) and become something less. *72*

The deed is very fresh; but already he regrets it. *73*

Overview: other things to note

Setting
o   There are several references in this scene to things happening off-stage. *'Hark!' (line 2)* is the first of them. List the others. They have the effect of heightening the drama, since they give us a strong sense of ongoing events close at hand.

Character
o   Macbeth: diminished
o   Lady Macbeth: enlarged, but with some weaknesses showing through

Action
o   The several voices (Macbeth's and Lady Macbeth's included) which describe, and mark, these terrible events

Style
o   Disjointed, confused – like the events themselves

Ideas
o   The intermingled colours of our human existence – black (deceitfulness), red (murder), gold (kingship), white (cowardice), green (the sea, the expanses of the world – which we can taint for all their vastness)

General
o   Does the murder of Duncan happen too early in the story?

Student Response

The attention we have paid to the voices of the scene has provoked interest. Some of the voices (the owl's, the crickets', the sleepers') 'stand for' (suggest) things beyond themselves and are in that sense symbolic, the class think.

'But then *plays* are symbolic – they tell stories which have something to say about life in general' They have been noticing the significant (i.e. symbolic) things that are said and done as well as the play's symbolic objects (bells, drums, daggers). We think up an essay question:

'Plays both tell stories and make statements.'

By what theatrical means do plays you have read make statements?

Symbols are a very important means by which statements are made or ideas underlined.

*****

There's some discussion of Macbeth's heart-searching, which has perhaps slowed the action down too much. But the general feeling is that things happen pretty quickly; and anyway we only understand the full meaning of what someone does if they or someone else has talked about it:

'Argument leading to action – the argument giving meaning to the action.'

How accurate a description is this of the plays you have studied? How important is it for a dramatist to maintain a balance between discussion and events?

*****

Act Two Scene Three

Commentary

When you've read the Porter's speech (with the help of the notes in your edition) and understand it reasonably well, try to say something about each of the following.

o   Its layout on the page
o   Its tone
o   The job it does as far as the storytelling is concerned

When you're planning a commentary try to give attention to some of its 'overarching' features, even if there are no questions directly about them. What are they, here?

> o   It's in prose, not verse. This is usual for 'low' characters, but here the porter's style of speech gives us some relief from the burning poetry and terse dialogue that has come before.
> o   It's humorous. Again, that provides relief. But it's also satirical in parts, and has something to say about one or two of the play's important themes.
> o   It allows time for the Macbeths to change into their night-clothes; and it provides suspense. Who, we wonder, is knocking, and why do they keep knocking and what will happen when they eventually get in?

Then there's the symbolic nature of the knocking. It's finding-out time. It's Judgement Day.

The Porter pretends (for his own amusement) to be keeping the gates of Hell. But he is, in a sense: the discovery that will soon be made is indeed hellish.

If this really were Hell he'd be kept busy, he says: there are plenty of people needing to be let in. We know one.

There are at least six sets of knockings on the gate. Why does he take so long to open it?

For the theatrical reasons we noted at the beginning. For the internal reasons that...

> o   he's drunk still, after the celebrations of the night before, and befuddled with sleep
> o   he's in a bad mood in spite of his jesting: he's pretty cynical in outlook to begin with, and it's very cold
> o   whoever is knocking will not reply to his demand that they identify themselves. (But he lets them in anyway.)

He's somebody else who doesn't do his job too well.

He imagines three people arriving at the gate of Hell to be admitted. What do they have in common? *3-13*

> Two were greedy, all three deceitful in different ways.

He gives up – it's too cold. If he'd had more time he'd have found a candidate for Hell, he says, from each of the professions. His general theme seems to be that we can all of us find that our *'primrose way'* (a path that looks attractive) takes us to Hell. Macbeth knows that, now. | *14-15*

The doors to Duncan's chamber were open *(Scene Two line 5)* to allow Murder to enter; now as the gate to the castle itself is unbarred we are aware that this dark place is about to be illuminated by the light of day, and if not of truth then at least of inquiry. More symbolism. And we can if we want find in it an extra (Shakespearean) reason why it was so hard to get the gate opened. | *18*

The exchange between Macduff and the Porter delays things a little longer and it looks wryly at what is happening to Macbeth. Alcohol is seen as another equivocator: it promises then denies (like the Witches). It seems to 'make' (empower) a man then it mars (unmakes, damages) him. | *27*

The Porter has struggled with the alcohol he drank and which incapacitated him; and he has succeeded in throwing off its effects (perhaps by throwing up – 'casting'). The heady wine of ambition, which disabled Macbeth's reason and made Lady Macbeth *'bold'* to the point of recklessness, is longer-lasting in its consequences. | *33-35*

Why does Macbeth choose to come to the castle entrance rather than stay in his room and wait for the murder to be discovered? (Or, rather, why does Shakespeare arrange things that way?)

'Noble...worthy': ? | *39,40*

Macbeth's speech in these next few lines is noticeably terse (brief and to the point), indicating his...

> anxiety, tenseness.

When he has to say a little more *('The labour...pain')* his words are stiff and conventional. Then he's short again *('This is the door')*. | *45* *46*

He's struggling with his awful knowledge, trying to maintain an air of normality while knowing that in a moment anything can happen. His brief answer to Lenox's question is not enough: he cannot stop the qualification coming out – *'He did appoint so'*. It's as if he is trying to avoid being caught out in an inaccuracy. Note the past tense *'did'* and compare the phrase with his earlier one *('tomorrow, as he purposes', Act One Scene Five line 58)*. | *48*

For a brief discussion of Lenox's speech see <u>Setting</u> below. | *49-56*

''Twas a rough night': terse, still; but he is soon to be garrulous. | *57*

The difficulty of naming evil deeds. Macbeth and Lady Macbeth have both encountered that. To name something is to acknowledge it. | *60-61*

'Confusion': just what Lenox has hoped (in *line 53*) the signs in the countryside would not foretell. The word's meaning here is strong – it implies a total breakdown of the natural order, chaos. The concept is personified, just as the *'horror'* of *lines 60-61* has been. The idea is reinforced by the religious references: it is the natural order of things as established by God that has been disrupted. This is a sin within a sin: Duncan's bed-chamber, where according to all the laws of hospitality he should have been secure, has been entered; and then the holy temple of his body has been broken into and his life stolen. | *62* *63-65*

Macbeth must appear slow to understand. Lenox is hardly any swifter. The slowed pace of the discovery is dramatically effective. | *65*

The 'Gorgon': we may subconsciously associate it with Lady Macbeth and the Witches, powerful female forces which have immobilised Macbeth's human nature (with their words rather than their stare).

67-68

Macduff's alarm, with its references to an imminent Judgement Day, is a call to the whole world to witness this atrocity: he names everyone of importance still sleeping except Lady Macbeth. But she comes anyway. Would she have dared stay away?

69

Lady Macbeth's *'trumpet'* image, and *'parley'* suggest war. Here it is a war between the forces of light and dark; soon it will be a war on the ground.

Macduff did not call for Lady Macbeth, and does not think she should know what is happening: as a woman she lacks the strength to survive the knowledge. Irony? She faints in a moment: maybe Macduff has put that idea into her head (but see discussion).

80

Macduff's grief seems heartfelt. Not so Macbeth's when he expresses it, as we shall see. What about Lady Macbeth's?

82-83

'Our house': is there something of the outrage here of a hostess whose standards of hospitality or cleanliness have been called into question? She would be expected as a woman to respond to the domestic rather than the political implications.

84

'Too cruel anywhere': Banquo, typically, takes the wider view.

This is a speech made (by Shakespeare) to be seen through. Its elaborateness make it suspect, as if he has rehearsed what he was going to say. But we can penetrate it in a more important sense. At a level deeper than that of his public reaction to the murder Macbeth realises that nothing will ever be the same again. This powerful speech looks forward to some of his most moving declarations near the end of the play. It's as if in speaking a falsehood (he is devastated by the event) he is speaking a truth (he is devastated by what the event has shown him. Life is meaningless).

87-92

Take the speech at face value and analyse its rhetorical effect.

- o   Repetition: *'had...had'*
- o   Antithesis (emphasised by the repetition)
- o   *'this instant'*: the immediacy of what has happened – it's as if it is still happening
- o   *'toys'*: belittles what he has done. 'He who dies with the most toys, wins.'
- o   The wine image remembers both his hospitality and his ambition: both have been poured away, leaving only bitter dregs which only a foolish man would boast about. More centrally, however, he refers to the richness of life, which has come to an end. The vault where he stored both the wine he offered his guests and his hidden ambition has become the vault of heaven (Creation) which no longer holds anything of value. (Images can have both central and associated meanings.)

'You are [amiss] and do not know't': again he speaks a greater truth than he should; everyone will know what he means.

93

He then backpedals somewhat, explaining that he is referring only to the fact that their father is dead, not to their future (or lack of it) as his successors. But he is over-emphatic – he uses four separate words which mean the same.

94-95

He's lucky – Macduff steps in to say the thing plainly and cover the awkward moment.   *96*

He's lucky, too, that Lenox supports him and prepares the way for the news that Macbeth killed the grooms. So far things are going not too badly.

But Lenox's *'as it seemed'* briefly suggests that there is some doubt about the grooms' guilt. They   *97*
were killed, he says, not because they had murdered Duncan but because they were dangerous.   *100-101*

Malcolm has already seemed suspicious in his reaction to the news that his father has been murdered –
his first need was to know who did it *(line 96)*. Macduff is equally alert to the possibilities and   *104*
challenges Macbeth.

Macbeth's defence is rambling and unconvincing. He was driven to kill the grooms (irrationally, he
admits) by the strength of his love for Duncan. Alright. But he goes on to over-dramatise the event –   *105*
'Here' – and paints a fanciful picture of Duncan's body ('paints' is right – look at the colours) with   *108*
some disturbing details – *'gashed stabs'* . The idea of the stab wounds as breaches in a defensive wall   *110*
through which *'ruin'* can enter repeats Macduff's image in *lines 63-65*; but it *does* repeat it, and
Macbeth seems to be copying.

'Steeped in the colours of their trade': he exaggerates their guilt – there is no evidence that they were   *112*
habitual murderers (and they would hardly have been set to guard the king if they had been. At no
point is there any discussion of a possible motive, apart from the fact that they were *'distracted'* and
may have been driven by madness).

'Breached' is an awkward term – 'wrapped in blood instead of being placed in their leather sheaths',   *113*
and it draws attention again to the fact that the grooms have not even taken the trouble to wipe their
knives.

His speech doesn't work. So Lady Macbeth faints. There's a wonderful stage opportunity for a hanging
pause before she does so.

But does she do it to cover up for Macbeth? Probably. Don't, however, discount the possibility that she
is, even though unexpectedly, overwhelmed by the tension of the moment. Her later descent into
madness shows that she is not beyond the reach of ordinary human ills.

Her fainting fit does in fact almost bring on a reaction against Macbeth. It allows Malcolm and   *117-123*
Donalbain an opportunity to discuss making what in all likelihood would be an accusation.

Donalbain however counsels caution: There may be hidden danger nearby (in a small hole drilled into
the earth – a snake, maybe, like the one under the flower that Lady Macbeth wanted her husband to
become?) They are not yet ready either to grieve or to take action other than a swift departure.

Banquo, however, does seem to offer a warning to Macbeth. Those who have been awakened need to
put on warm clothes instead of their nightgowns…but maybe he is suggesting that armour would be   *124*
more appropriate for them all, since their *'frailties'* are 'exposed' to whoever has killed Duncan. Then
they will investigate the murder. And he himself, although he is afraid and suspicious (he has
'scruples' – reservations – about what he has heard) will stand against treachery.

Everyone (Macbeth included?) echoes his words. Macbeth repeats Banquo's suggestion that they dress   *129*
more appropriately (in armour?) It's important for him to identify himself with the group.

The two men who are now most in danger are left alone on stage. Flight is their wisest course of action.
But there's also a touch of moral condemnation in *'Let's not consort with them.'* They have heard one   *133*

person too many express false grief at the death of their father.

'Daggers in men's smiles': remember *'There's no art to find...'*

'The near in blood, the nearer bloody': they are at great risk because they are nearest in blood to Duncan. But Macbeth is also *'near in blood'*, in two senses, and therefore a threat to them.   *139-140*

Some commentators have been concerned that *'the shaft that's shot'* (fired from Macbeth's crossbow?) has in fact landed (in Duncan), so what Malcolm is saying here doesn't really make sense. But Malcolm is suggesting that the shaft may have passed through Duncan and is now headed towards *them*, with enough impetus to be still *'murderous'*.

In a situation like this you must be prepared to be flexible in your principles. Running away without   *141-144*
saying goodbye ('shifting') may seem cowardly (and may look suspicious – 'shifty'); but the world is merciless, as they have just seen, and self-preservation must therefore override other considerations.

Overview: other things to note

Setting
o   We are wholly immersed in Macbeth's predicament in this scene; but there's more to the story than what happens to Macbeth, Shakespeare reminds us in Lenox's speech *(lines 49-56)*...and we draw back a little. More voices, this time in the countryside around; an image of burning *('combustion')*; the owl again; an earthquake. The impression we have had since Macbeth's victory is that everything in the country at large is now fine, and it is a time for celebration and the strengthening of bonds. But Lenox tells us that this is still a *'woeful time'*, that the cost of revolt is still being weighed, and that the last thing Scotland needs now is confusion and *'new-hatch'd'* trouble.

Character
o   Macbeth: not good in a tight situation
o   Lady Macbeth: better, but of limited help to him
o   Banquo: a standard by which, and a man by whom, Macbeth may be judged.
o   Malcolm and Donalbain: hardly distinguishable. Neither seems to suspect the other.
o   The Porter: his comic functionality; his cynicism (if you know Robert Bolt's play *A Man For all Seasons*, you'll see a similarity with the Common Man). Who's the Porter talking to, to begin with, by the way?

Action
o   Only Macbeth and Lenox go to view the body, after Macduff has discovered it. There are good (dramatic) reasons why they should: Macbeth is able to dispose of the grooms, but that action throws suspicion on him. Lenox is used to present the evidence against the grooms, but he does so with reservations. The complexities of the situation are thus emphasised.

Style
o   The more passionate the language, the more suspicious we should be of it – a lesson for the modern world. Set greater store by the quirky prose of the Porter: he has little to lose or gain by his words and seeks only to amuse himself.

Ideas
o   Reality transcends words: the deed cannot be named, and Macduff says that Macbeth and Lenox must see Duncan's body for themselves.
o   (Linked idea): life is full of contradictions, but some things (the fact of death) cannot be contradicted *(lines 85)*.
o   Life is full of contradictions; and some of them can only be resolved by action *(lines105-106)*.
General
o   Where are we in the *shape* of the play?

Student Response

'Why do some lines have more than one possible meaning? And why do some things that happen have more than one explanation? Shakespeare should have told us why Lady Macbeth fainted.'

Some questions are best answered with questions (one of Lady M's tactics).

> *'When we are not exactly sure what the words or the events of a play mean, we should see that as an opportunity rather than a problem.'*

> *What opportunities for interpretation have you found in the texts of your chosen plays? How can that freedom strengthen rather than weaken a play's impact?*

That would be an interesting essay to tackle, the class decide. It would involve identifying some of the play's ambiguous words, statements and actions (there are plenty) and showing how different readings of them throw differing light on the situation. There's also additional material here for an answer to the question earlier about how dramatists bring the audience closer to the play – by making them struggle with its meaning, in this case.

It might, of course, be possible to see ambiguity as a failure to communicate properly.

*****

The class are interested in the timing of events. When Banquo and Fleance enter at the beginning of *Act Two* we hear that it is past midnight – but probably not by much. Macbeth and Banquo have a brief conversation. Macbeth, once he is alone, tells us that Lady Macbeth is already working on the grooms. He sends a message that she should ring a bell when everything is safe. After his soliloquy he leaves to kill Duncan. We have to assume he goes straight there. When Lady Macbeth enters in *Scene Two* he is *'about it'* and when he himself comes in the deed is done. They are interrupted by the knocking on the gate. The Porter seems to have been asleep (he did not go to bed until after the party and the *'second cock'* – gone 3.00 am). What has happened to the several hours in between?

We talk about dramatic compression and expansion, and (once more) theatrical effect. What in the end matters is audience perception.

> *'Plays are illusions but they seek to make reality plain.'*

> *Show how dramatists you have studied attempt to create believable illusion on the stage but use that illusion to say things about real life.*

Our conclusions: the more often we watch plays the more practised we become in accepting dramatic conventions which breach the laws of chronology or logic or physics, or the principle of historical accuracy. What should not be violated, however, are the basic truths of human nature. Stage characters must behave like 'real' people within a representation of the human condition which is internally consistent and matches, in its essence, the world as we know it. That is the 'reality' which must be made plain.

The simple reality here is that a terrible murder has been committed by an ambitious man urged on by his even more ambitious wife. Just how long the murder takes doesn't matter too much. The illusion is that the events have spanned a whole night. That illusion is created in part by the many references to things that mark the passing of the hours (we listed some of them as the off-stage events of *Scene Two*).

*****

That leads to another question:

> *'Time in a play is very different from time on the wrist watch we may consult in the darkness of the theatre.'*

How is theatrical time different from 'real' time?

There's also an opportunity here to discuss the difference between what happens when we watch a play in the theatre on the one hand, and read it in a book or study it in class on the other. We need to remember that a dramatist does not write to be read, and that he can expect to get away with things on a stage that may seem absurd on the printed page. (Poor novelists sometimes do the same in reverse…)

*****

Act Two Scene Four

Commentary Practice

Let's treat this whole scene as if it's the basis of a examination commentary question. It's not a lot more promising than the last passage we selected – in fact the scene is often omitted in productions of the play – but part of the art of writing commentaries is learning to 'make much of little'.

On the next page you'll find the passage set out as on an exam paper. This time it has not been marked, but a set of notes has been added on a separate page. Try to match up the notes with details from the passage: in other words do your own underlining of the words and phrases you think the notes are based on. This will give you practice in searching the text for yourself, with some guidance as to what you're looking for.

You can then, if you wish, go ahead and write the commentary.

Just in case you can't find all the quotations, the matching line references are given at the end of the book. Try not to use that list until you've done your best to find the quotes yourself.

Practice Commentary 2

Sample passage

Enter ROSS, with an OLD MAN.

OLD MAN: Threescore and ten I can remember well;
        Within the volume of which time, I have seen
        Hours dreadful and things strange, but this sore night
        Hath trifled former knowings.
ROSS: Ha, good father,
        Thou seest, the heavens, as troubled with man's act,   *5*
        Threatens his bloody stage: by th' clock 'tis day,
        And yet dark night strangles the travelling lamp.
        Is't night's predominance, or the day's shame,
        That darkness does the face of earth entomb,
        When living light should kiss it?
OLD MAN: 'Tis unnatural,   *10*
        Even like the deed that's done. On Tuesday last,
        A falcon towering in her pride of place,
        Was by a mousing owl hawk'd at, and kill'd.
ROSS: And Duncan's horses (a thing most strange and certain)
        Beauteous and swift, the minions of their race,   *15*
        Turned wild in nature, broke their stalls, flung out,
        Contending 'gainst obedience, as they would make
        War with mankind.
OLD MAN: 'Tis said, they ate each other.
        ROSS: They did so, to th' amazement of mine eyes,
        That look'd upon't.

Enter MACDUFF

           Here comes the good Macduff. –   *20*
        How goes the world, Sir, now?
MACDUFF: Why, see you not?
ROSS: Is't known who did this more than bloody deed?
MACDUFF: Those that Macbeth hath slain.
ROSS: Alas, the day!
        What good could they pretend?
MACDUFF: They were suborned.
        Malcolm and Donalbain, the King's two sons,   *25*
        Are stol'n away and fled; which puts upon them
        Suspicion of the deed.
ROSS: 'Gainst Nature still;
        Thriftless Ambition, that wilt ravin up
        Thine own life's means – then 'tis most like,
        The sovereignty will fall upon Macbeth.   *30*
MACDUFF: He is already nam'd, and gone to Scone
        To be invested.
ROSS: Where is Duncan's body?
MACDUFF: Carried to Colme-hill,
        The sacred storehouse of his predecessors,

         And guardian of their bones.

ROSS: Will you to Scone?   *35*

MACDUFF: No cousin, I'll to Fife.

ROSS: Well, I will thither.

MACDUFF: Well may you see things well done there: – adieu,
         Lest our old robes sit easier than our new.

ROSS: Farewell, father.

OLD MAN: God's benison go with you; and with those   *40*
         That would make good of bad, and friends of foes.

                                          [*Exeunt*

Guiding question

> *How does this passage help the audience understand both the themes of the play and the forward movement of the plot?*

Look at that guiding question closely. It's really in two parts…

o   What does the passage tell us about the play's themes?
o   What does the passage tell us about how the plot is progressing?

No, it's really in three parts, if you look again. That word 'How?' is important. It's different from 'What?' and will give you a chance to say something about Shakespeare's methods in the passage – more interesting than just a list of the things the passage tells us.

Add underlining and notes as before. It's up to you whether you actually write the commentary. It's up to you also whether you look at the sample underlining and notes (on the page following the passage) before or after you've written it.

Sample passage with underlining

We'll add line numbers and three underline styles to help you in your searching:

Shakespeare's methods
Themes
Plot

Enter ROSS, with an OLD MAN.

OLD MAN:	Threescore and ten I can remember well;	
	Within the volume of which time, I have seen	
	Hours dreadful and things strange, but this sore night	
	hath trifled former knowings.	
ROSS:	Ha, good father,	
	Thou seest, the heavens, as troubled with man's act,	5
	Threatens his bloody stage: by th' clock 'tis day,	
	And yet dark night strangles the travelling lamp.	
	Is't night's predominance, or the day's shame,	
	That darkness does the face of earth entomb,	
	When living light should kiss it?	
OLD MAN:	'Tis unnatural,	10
	Even like the deed that's done. On Tuesday last,	
	A falcon towering in her pride of place,	
	Was by a mousing owl hawk'd at, and kill'd.	
ROSS:	And Duncan's horses (a thing most strange and certain)	
	Beauteous and swift, the minions of their race,	15
	Turned wild in nature, broke their stalls, flung out,	
	Contending 'gainst obedience, as they would make	
	War with mankind.	
OLD MAN:	'Tis said, they ate each other.	
ROSS:	They did so, to th' amazement of mine eyes,	
	That look'd upon't.	

Enter MACDUFF

	Here comes the good Macduff. –	20
	How goes the world, Sir, now?	
MACDUFF:	Why, see you not?	
ROSS:	Is't known who did this more than bloody deed?	
MACDUFF:	Those that Macbeth hath slain.	
ROSS:	Alas, the day!	
	What good could they pretend?	
MACDUFF:	They were suborned.	
	Malcolm and Donalbain, the King's two sons,	25
	Are stol'n away and fled; which puts upon them	
	Suspicion of the deed.	
ROSS:	'Gainst Nature still;	
	Thriftless Ambition, that wilt ravin up	
	Thine own life's means – then 'tis most like,	
	The sovereignty will fall upon Macbeth.	30
MACDUFF:	He is already nam'd, and gone to Scone	
	To be invested.	

ROSS: Where is Duncan's body?
MACDUFF: Carried to Colme-hill,
      The sacred storehouse of his predecessors,
      And guardian of their bones.
ROSS: Will you to Scone?   *35*
MACDUFF: No cousin, I'll to Fife.
ROSS: Well, I will thither.
MACDUFF: Well may you see things well done there: – adieu,
      Lest our old robes sit easier than our new.
ROSS: Farewell, father.
OLD MAN: God's benison go with you: and with those   *40*
      That would make good of bad, and friends of foes.
                                                    [*Exeunt*

Sample notes

Shakespeare's methods:
o   (1) Uses old man to tell what is happening in the country in general.
o   (2) Old man's credentials (age and experience) established (compare role etc. of Porter)
o   (4) Emphasises unusualness of events
o   (19-20) Ross an eye-witness of events
o   (21) Brings on Macduff with up-to-date news

Themes:
o   (6) Life as a kind of drama
o   (6-7) Disorientation– is it night or day?
o   (10-11) Unnaturalness
o   (16) Revolt against obedience
o   (18) Species preying on itself
o   (28) Ambition
o   (34) The sanctity of kingship

Plot *(We used the word 'plot' rather than 'story' to draw your attention to the shape of the action.)*
o   Macbeth's fortunes seem to be on the rise; but there are signs here that things may turn around…
o   The general unease in the community (as evidenced by the Old Man)
o   (5) Heaven's reaction against what has happened
o   (20) Macduff's position in the play as a 'good' man
o   (25-27) The fact that Malcolm and Donalbain have escaped– a threat to Macbeth
o   (31-32) Macbeth is about to be crowned
o   Macduff's refusal to go to Macbeth's coronation (36) – a threat to Macbeth
o   (38) The fear that their new king may be harsher than their old one
o   The idea that there are good forces (and forces of reconciliation, note) still in play.

Overall observation to round off your commentary (it's always good to have one of those):

o   The important information about what's happening comes towards the end of the scene, as Shakespeare prepares us for the next part of the story.

Additional questions (A Level)

    1. How are the seeds of further conflict sown in Act Two of 'Macbeth'?

    2. Analyse the elements of suspense in Act Two of 'Macbeth'.

A Level Questions: An Overview

This is probably a good point at which to say something about the different types of GCE A Level question candidates may face, and the relationships among them. Be aware, of course, that assessment requirements regarding types of question (rubrics) differ among examining bodies, and change with changes of syllabus.

1. The Context Question. This is much the same as the commentary tasks we set at the end of *Act One* and *Act Two*. Candidates are given a printed passage from the chosen work and asked to write about it, either with or without guiding questions. Analysis of the passage needs to be complete and very detailed. Guiding questions may focus on any of the five features we have used as the basis for our concluding notes on individual scenes – Setting, Character, Action, Style and Ideas. Some examiners will ask the candidate to outline his or her own response to the passage, or to speculate about an audience's *likely* response. There may also be a question about Elizabethan times, or about the theory and practice of drama – based, again, on the printed passage. Some WJEC (Welsh Joint Education Committee) and OCR (Oxford, Cambridge and RSA) questions are of this type.

2. The Passage-Based Question (normally used in open-book exams). Candidates are instructed to look back at a passage in the play, or sometimes at a complete scene, and use it as a starting point for an essay on one of the play's wider aspects. Here's an example of a *Macbeth* question of that sort, one based on the scene we have just studied. The question is in the style of an EDEXCEL question.

    Look again at Act 2, Scene 4. By a careful analysis of this scene, consider the importance of Elizabethan beliefs about nature, order and kingship in helping us understand the play as a whole.

3. The Multiple-Passage-Based Question (some AQA questions are of this type). This asks candidates to consider linked passages from different parts of the work, and to consider the relationship among them or the contribution they make, overall, to the effect of the play. Here is an example:

    Discuss episodes in 'Macbeth' in which unusual or supernatural events occur or are described. How do they add to the play's significance and impact?

4. The Essay Question (with guidance). This does not direct the candidate to a particular part of the play, but may indicate some of the areas of the essay topic the candidate is expected to cover, for example:
- o   the setting, characters, action, style and ideas of the play (in relation to the topic)
- o   the candidate's (or audience's) response to the topic
- o   the background against which Shakespeare wrote.

 The following example is along the lines of an OCR question, and you will see that it asks in part for a consideration of the same topic as 1-3 above.

    'The play is in part about Man's (and Woman's) desire to remake the world as they would like it to be.'
    How far do you agree with this view of 'Macbeth'? In your answer you should:
- o   *discuss characters and their motives, as well as Shakespeare's handling of narrative development and setting in the play;*
- o   *give your own response to the critical view expressed, weighing how far you can agree with it and why;*
- o   *show an understanding of Elizabethan beliefs about creation and the world order.*

5. The Essay Question (without guidance). Example:

Discuss Shakespeare's use of The Supernatural in 'Macbeth'.

We have set these five types of question side by side so that you can become aware of one further thing.

All questions, from the narrowest to the broadest (Numbers 1 and 5 as we have given them), derive from the details of the text. So your preparation for the exam (whichever exam it is) must largely consist of getting to know those details very thoroughly, and learning to judge their significance. All of the practice commentaries we have included will help you to do that.

Act Three

Act Three Scene One

Commentary

Banquo imagines he is addressing Macbeth; but he is not experiencing a vision – he's much too sound of mind for that. This speech does, however, prepare us for its frightening parallel later in the act, when Macbeth sees the ghost of Banquo and talks to it.

1

Banquo speaks the three titles in the reverse order in which they were acquired. But he doesn't name Macbeth the man: it's as if he has become invisible under his honours.

'Weird women' – they are less than supernatural forces in his reckoning; and he diminishes their role in things *('it was said'*, not *'they said')*. But he gives them credit in a moment for the accuracy of their predictions. The alliteration of *'w...w'* prepares us for *'fear...foully'* (echoing the *'fair...foul'* of the opening scenes of the play). We are back where we started – but a lot has happened in between.

2

Banquo is contemplating what the future may hold for him. The Witches did after all promise that his sons would be kings.

3

o   Is he revealing that he too could be driven by ambition, and so therefore no better than Macbeth? Has he thereby fallen into the trap he warned Macbeth about – allowing himself to be misled by *'trifles'*? He does seems willing to view the Witches in a more positive light – *'truth...shine...verities...oracles...hope'.* Some commentators have found here a flaw in his character, or, alternatively, some inconsistency in Shakespeare's presentation of him.

6-10

o   Or are these just the musings of a man whose mind is momentarily freed from other things while he waits for someone to arrive? (It's been suggested that he is here to get permission from Macbeth to go riding. Might that have started him thinking?)

Even if he does harbour royal ambitions he could not, to attain them, take the kind of action he suspects Macbeth of; so he remains a useful dramatic and moral counterpoint to the play's central figure.

He realises he must take care.

10

King Macbeth and his wife are announced by trumpets and are presumably wearing crowns. What was about to happen at the end of *Act Two* has indeed happened: here is the visual proof, in case Banquo's opening words were not clear enough.

They speak, clearly, so that Banquo can overhear them: they're making a bit of a fuss of him – ominous in itself, but not as ominous, in the light of later events, as the phrase *'a gap in our great feast'.*

13

Much of what now goes on looks forward to the banqueting scene. How can that matter to us as an audience, since the episode comes later?

Many of the people watching the play in Macbeth's time would already know the story; many would have seen the play more than once. They would be able to pick up on the forward references and grasp something of their sinister nature. What about the rest of us?

Well, some actors would be able to give us a sense that 'something's up' without speaking the significant lines significantly.

Then there's you. You aren't just audience you're scholars. You're allowed to look ahead, because you already know the play (don't you?), and see hidden meanings – even those that would be hidden from a first-time audience. (Is it possible to hear an echo before you hear the sound itself? Interesting question.) You may want to read the scene again before you start this next section of the Commentary and pick out the examples of double-entendre – 'things heard twice, in different ways' (words or statements with a double meaning, one of them often more significant than the other) – for yourself.

So the supper will be *'solemn'*. It will indeed, for Macbeth; and Banquo will indeed be there.   *14-15*

How do you read Banquo's reply? He makes a formal statement of allegiance to Macbeth. Is that because he
o   knows he needs to avoid arousing the suspicion that he is suspicious?
o   is, through his coldness, showing his distrust of Macbeth even while going through the motions of accepting him as king?
o   genuinely willing to support Macbeth because he *is*, now, the king?

We can't be sure that Macbeth cares. He has already made up his mind that Banquo should die and has already begun to make arrangements for that to happen. So his friendly enquiry, *'Ride you this*   *19* *afternoon?'* means more than it appears to; and it means more than Banquo realises, in spite of his caution, or he wouldn't have gone.

Much else of what Macbeth says to Banquo is designed to reassure him. But the more he reassures Banquo the more we, the audience, mistrust him; and that's before he tells us what he's thinking. Shakespeare has the knack of making us 'know ahead'. The very mention of the *'night'* through which Banquo may need to ride for a *'dark hour or twain'* sets off alarm bells: night has such dreadful   *26-27* associations in the play.

Macbeth has already decided to dispose of Banquo; but that does not stop him from sounding him out   *29-32* about Malcolm and Donalbain and the accusations they are laying against him. Why?

---

o   He wants to know how far the accusations have spread and whether subjects like Banquo will have paid them any attention.
o   This is part of his strategy to reassure Banquo, by, here, appearing to take him into his confidence and promising to seek his advice the next day *(lines 32-34)*.
o   Or both.

The Macbeth we see in this scene is much more confident, much more skilled, and quickly becoming more practised in subterfuge.

Both Banquo and Fleance *are* 'called upon' – as part of Macbeth's plan.   *36*

And even this farewell rings – not hollow, but significantly: it has a *double* ring to it.

Look how smoothly Macbeth gives himself space for his plotting.   *40-43*

Preparations are already under way. When he says *'those men'* the Attendant knows exactly who he   *44* means; and the assassins are already waiting at the gate.   *46*

Macbeth's next soliloquy would make a better commentary passage than the ones we've (deliberately)   *47-71* chosen so far; so we'll save it for that and you can tackle it when we've finished our work on the rest of *Act Three*. That will allow us to rattle through the rest of this scene fairly quickly: it's largely 'practical' stuff, i.e. to do with the mechanics of manipulation and murder (none the less absorbing for

67

that to an Elizabethan audience).

The Attendant is given a job by Macbeth; but he is also given one by Shakespeare – to ensure that we know there's plotting afoot.   *72*

This speech is largely for the audience's sake – we weren't at yesterday's meeting. But it's also for Macbeth's: he needs to be sure he has convinced these men; and it's maybe for theirs too: they are not of the brightest and perhaps Macbeth feels he needs to remind them of his arguments.   *74*

'Which, you thought, had been our innocent self': has he been training them up for this, keeping them oppressed so that he could then use them as agents against Banquo, or indeed anybody else who gave him trouble? Or is it just that he has already turned brutal toward some of his subjects?   *77-78*

Note the organisation of his summary, which presumably reflects the organisation of the speech he made to them the day before. He is going to be an efficient tyrant.

'Half a soul, and...a notion crazed': is this how he actually sees each of the men?   *82*

He holds the name of their tormentor to the end (even though they already know it) for rhetorical effect), and puts it into their own mouths.

These 'half-souls' have little to say for themselves: they are of the world's malcontents, and need very little setting-on.

'Our point of second meeting': he is more than efficient, he is business-like.   *85*

But his concerns are evident in *'his issue'* (a bit out of place): it is Banquo's offspring as much as Banquo himself that Macbeth must take care of.   *88*

'To the grave' (towards the grave): they are half-dead with despair (but remember what happens to them).   *89*

'Beggared yours' (ruined your family, *your* offspring): Macbeth plays on their envy and anger as well as their desperation.

They are men; men can take only so much abuse; they are ready to fight back.   *90*

Macbeth is expansive. He has the leisure, the confidence, the authority to speak at length about anything he chooses; and they must listen while he questions what kind of men they are. Now that he is at the head of the *'valued file'* (the hierarchy) he can question others' place in it. And if these men count themselves better than the lowest of the low, and are willing to act in Macbeth's (and their own) interest, he will love them. He promises. These dogs, these half-souls.   *91*

105

And then he reveals a weakness. This health, this security, this confidence are only apparent, something he 'wears', like a cloak. Beneath it he is ailing, for fear of Banquo.

The two men complement each other. One is enraged, the other is worn down. Both are reckless.   *107-113*

And both, says Macbeth again, have an enemy in Banquo (*'was'* implies 'and still is').   *113-114*

He has won their confidence, and can now cement it by confiding in them further. He tries to recover from his earlier admission that he felt weakened by Banquo, and asserts that he could of course simply kill him openly because he has decided it is necessary and justified. But there are political reasons   *117* against such a public act. So he has turned to these two men to help him. But he is deliberately vague about what these *'sundry and weighty'* political reasons are. We know they are less political than superstitious; but he can not tell them that. *125*

'Your spirits shine through you': *127*
o   'You are fine, spirited men: anybody can see that.'
o   'You are transparent, and I know just what you're made of.'

Not only stars shine.

Macbeth has more research to do (how? Banquo has already left). For the puzzling phrase *'spy o''* read *129* 'information about', and don't worry about the mysterious third murderer until he appears.

He wants his hired assassins to make a flawless job of *'the work'*, as if he's asked them to make a piece *133* of furniture. That seems unlikely: you can't get the help, you know (think of the Grooms and the Porter).

He still shies away from calling a spade a spade, a murder a murder: Fleance's death will be just an *'absence'*. Is this the euphemism (roundabout way of speaking) of *135*
o   a schemer and manipulator (killing a child might have been more than even these two wretches could face), or
o   a man who will not yet fully acknowledge what he is doing?

'That dark hour' is the same *'dark hour or twain'* Banquo said he might have to borrow to get home. *137* They will be his for good, and he will not make it back.

'Concluded' suggests both the completion of a carefully-laid plan and satisfaction at how well it has *been* laid.

Overview: other things to note

<u>Setting</u>

o   This is the royal palace – the castle at Forres. Macbeth has attired himself in more than kingly clothes.
o   There is some normality at Court: there is to be a feast; Banquo has leisure to go off riding.
o   But *does* he have to ask permission first? And *has* Macbeth oppressed the two men he now seeks help from? Is that the kind of court he has established?

<u>Character</u>

o   Macbeth: one minute the concerned host and ally, the next a dangerous enemy; a paranoid fearful of his position, then an efficient schemer then a bully then a confidant and finally an employer concerned about how well the job will be done. Macbeth is several things in this scene, and something different again in the next.
o   Lady Macbeth: contributes little; we'll find out why in a moment.
o   Banquo: some question-marks over his character; but dramatically Shakespeare needs him to be seen as a martyr to Macbeth's paradoxical ambition and insecurity, and so would be unlikely to suggest that he is himself ambitious.

<u>Action</u>
o   Urgency: *'Within this hour at most' line 127…'tonight' (line 130)…'anon' (line 137)… 'straight' (line 139)*

<u>Style</u>
o   How Macbeth's style differs according to who he's speaking to

o   The question *(lines 140-141)*, already raised four times in the play, of what happens to a man after he dies

General
o   Is what Macbeth plans here worse or better than his murder of Duncan? (You'll need to begin by thinking about what 'worse' and 'better' might mean.) The question is really, 'Does Shakespeare want us to be more shocked by this killing than we were by the earlier one?' You're being asked to make a theatrical rather than a moral judgement.

Student Response

The class are still a bit worried by all of these references forward to which their attention has been drawn (by such phrases as, 'what's going to happen', 'becomes significant', 'in the light of later events' and 'foreshadows'). They accept that as readers and re-readers of the play they are in a way privileged, and can see things a theatre audience would be unlikely to notice.

'But how much of the irony is intended and how much of it accidental?'

We list the all the examples of irony we can remember under three headings.
o   Unconscious or accidental linguistic irony *('It is a peerless kinsman')*
o   Deliberate linguistic irony, where the speaker is aware of a double meaning in what he or she is saying *('He that's coming must be provided for')*
o   The irony of events (by trying to get more Macbeth loses all). This irony is more fundamental and is always 'accidental' (although the acts that bring it about can be deliberate) – unless you believe in a Creator who arranges things that way.

As far as this present scene is concerned we must decide
o   how much of what Macbeth says, to Banquo in particular but also once or twice to the assassins, carries an extra meaning of which he is aware
o   how much of his dialogue is word-playing of a self-congratulatory and almost sadistic kind.

How much of what is said, moreover, is an indication that Shakespeare is letting us into the secret of what is about to happen?

   'Irony is a means by which the dramatist involves his audience in the story he is telling.'

   Show how this process works in the plays you have studied.

We've decided that irony involves an audience by drawing them in, since it accords them a special relationship: they are allowed to know more than some if not all of the characters (but less than the dramatist). The dramatist confides in his audience, and thereby makes watching the play a very personalised, even intimate, experience.

Irony sometimes operates however at a more profound level. The dramatist creates an illusion on the stage, then encourages us to believe in it; but we never do, quite. We know the play is not 'really' real. Then, with a mixture of shock and horror (in some plays) we begin to understand that the story is not about other people, 'pretend' people or not: it's about us. So Oedipus (*Oedipus Rex*), the detective of his own crime, is us searching through the past for an understanding of the present. The sad and tattered figures of Estragon and Vladimir (*Waiting for Godot*) are us in our state of perpetual bewilderment. Willy Loman (*Death of a Salesman*) is us when our dreams turn out to be too massive for us to carry them any longer. And Macbeth taking a horrible delight in taunting Banquo before he sends him to his death is us in our worst playground moments, which we all too often carry with us into adulthood. So what has seemed illusion is real in a very fundamental way. This is another of drama's great ironies (tricks if you will) and it explains the terror which Aristotle saw as a being generated (alongside pity) by successful tragedy. We are all, potentially, as ambitious, and as cruel, and as self-destructive, as Macbeth.

A recent exam question asked candidates to examine ways in which the audience participates in a play. Another one took as its starting point the idea that audiences are accused, by modern plays at least. There are the beginnings of answers to both of those questions in the above discussion.

As readers of a play we are privileged; but we are also of course handicapped; and we go on to talk about what we're missing as we work our way slowly (very slowly, some of us say) from page to page of *Macbeth*.

*****

Act Three Scene Two

Commentary

Why does Shakespeare bring Lady Macbeth on alone at the beginning of this scene?

Another question may help you answer that first one. Can you see any connection between her query about Banquo and her speech in *lines 4-7*? Note that between the two she sends for Macbeth to talk to him about something. What?

Putting all three together, we can surmise that she also sees Banquo as a problem and wants to explore ways of dealing with him and thereby making their joy less *'doubtful' (line 8)*. But Banquo is her husband's best friend, so she will have to be careful. In the event she does not raise the matter.

What she doesn't know is that Macbeth is now ahead of her.

Lady Macbeth's lines sound proverbial. Is she beginning to face up to some very basic truths about the way things work (which is what proverbs are)? Is there some regret there that they ever started this thing?

4-7

She doesn't share any of that with Macbeth when he enters, however; and it's significant that each is now hiding something from the other.

Lady Macbeth, in fact, contradicts what she has just said. She denies her own misgivings (if that is what they are) and tells Macbeth that he should not be worrying about what has been done because it *has* been done and is now in the past. We can imagine that she is more concerned at the suspicion which his behaviour may arouse.

8-12

Macbeth's reply is rather disjointed. He begins by showing his insecurity: he is afraid of the repercussions of what they have done. Then he is defiant: he would rather see the whole world fall apart than live in fear of what may happen (there are reminders here of the recklessness of the two murderers). He moves on in the longest part of the speech to what seems almost envy of Duncan, who now sleeps peacefully.

13-15
16-19

19-26

The snake image carries with it the idea of a natural healing process which will allow the forces ranged against Macbeth to recover from the wound he has inflicted and turn on him. He is, in a sense, on the 'wrong' (the unnatural) side.

So it would suit him to have the *'frame of things'*, the whole structure of Creation, collapse. (As an alternative reading, he would be prepared to have life 'dis-jointed' from the after life, so that there is no possibility of survival after death – he'd *'jump the life to come'* in other words. You'll remember that he was willing to do that, in *Act Two Scene Seven line 7*, if it would guarantee his security.)

There's a contrast between the scale of that and the personal activities (eating, sleeping) he seeks to preserve – Macbeth has begun to shrink into a man who is mainly concerned with his own comforts, peace of mind and safety.

There's some self-indulgence in these ramblings, and some extravagance in the style…
o   alliteration (three examples)
o   personification (of the snake – *'it'* becomes *'she'*; of malice, perhaps; of treason)

o declarativeness *('But let the frame of things...')*
o strong images of fever *('affliction...shake')* and torture (*'to lie'* as on the rack)
o rhetorical compression: *'Better be with'*
o measured rhythms in the last five lines

Lady Macbeth tries to jolly (not bully, you'll note) him out of his mood. He should be *'bright'* (like a star) and *'jovial'* (which means god-like rather than just cheerful).   *26-29*

She is only briefly successful: he almost immediately turns again to his own insecurities: Banquo is a worry to him.   *29-31*

Why? He's just arranged to have him murdered. Is he
o just hedging his bets in case Banquo returns safely?
o attempting to conceal from Lady Macbeth his involvement in Banquo's death? (which would raise another 'Why?')

Macbeth's deeper concern is not with Banquo but with the fact that he is having to hide behind a mask (*'vizard'*). There is a basic indignity as well as dishonesty in that.   *32-35*

It's this kind of anguish which Lady Macbeth can not let him sink into. Her *'You must leave this'* (stop thinking like that) is rather more curt.

But he persists in seeking from her whatever sympathy she will give. The snake has become scorpions in his mind, poised to sting...or are they already stinging?   *36*

He himself raises again the matter which Lady Macbeth was perhaps going to – the danger presented by Banquo and his son.   *37*

They're not immortal, is her reply.   *38*

He already knew that; so there's a touch of pathos in the fact that he's now able to cheer himself up with the thought, just because it has come from her. It's as if he has sought some approval for what he has arranged, and he thinks he's just been given it. But he won't tell her exactly what he has done. There's something little-boyish about all of that: 'Mummy, what would you say if I told you that...?'   *39*

Shakespeare now decides to move on from the domesticity of this exchange to a higher level of intensity. Macbeth switches suddenly, after *'jocund'*, (light-hearted) to poetry the like of which we have heard so far only at some of the play's highest moments.   *40*

In the opening section we have a run of dark references culminating in a line made ominous by its vagueness and powerful by its alliteration and rhythm: *'There shall be done a deed of dreadful note.'*   *45*

He has virtually silenced his wife. This is a new, determined Macbeth, the kind of man she wanted him to be. But is she now afraid of him?

The intimacy of his response to her question is chilling: he is about to pull a plum out of the pie and impress his *'dearest chuck'* with it; but he wants it to be a surprise.   *46*

Then he turns away from her, probably physically as well as verbally. She has interrupted him in full flight. Here are some questions about this part of his speech.
o What does he not want *'pitiful day'* to see?
o What is *'that great bond'* which he wants cancelled?
o How does Banquo's existence keep him *'pale'*?

- How can light thicken?
- The crow is a reminder of the……image, which was a symbol of impending……
- *'droop and drowse'* suggests that the good things of day……
- *'night's black agents'*: he is thinking of……
- *'preys'* continues the……imagery

- The murder of Duncan and Fleance
- The contract, or lease, Banquo (and Fleance) have with life – in other words, their lives
- It makes him afraid, which turns his complexion white (sickly) – like the paper the *'bond'* is written on.
- By becoming darker (just an illusion of course) and more difficult to see through…and by association more viscous (like blood which will no longer be able to carry good feelings such as pity to the heart, as earlier in the play)
- raven…death
- are becoming sleepy and will be caught off-guard.
- his murderers? Himself? The Witches? An agent acts on behalf of somebody else. It's clear who the murderers are acting on behalf of; but Macbeth? The Witches?
- bird – suggesting not carrion birds (crows) now but birds of prey

---

Then he turns back to his wife. She is astounded, and it shows.

It is his turn to reassure *her*. In this part of the play Macbeth takes the lead. He offers her something which sounds like a proverb, but which expresses his reverse morality (two wrongs *do* make a right, to his way of thinking). Then he leads her off.

Overview: other things to note

Setting
'Another room' (stage directions): the palace holds a variety of rooms where different things can happen, different conversations take place, and secrecy is possible.

Character
- Macbeth: the conflict within him persists, but it's changed its character. It's not a struggle between right and wrong (which it was, once) but between fear and comfort.
- Lady Macbeth: diminishes in power as Macbeth increases.

Action
- Only in words – speculations, advice, reassurances, outcries, hints, invocations – a very mixed bag. The real action is taking place wherever Banquo is.

Style
- Also a mixed bag. Do the sharp swings from intimacy to rhetoric (and back again) and the sudden switches of audience (who Macbeth is talking to) call into question the sincerity of either the intimacy or the rhetoric?

Ideas
- The idea of *'courses'* of action: how one decision leads on to another of similar character, then another. That's part of the inevitability of tragedy – an important dramatic concept.

General
- Are there some cracks appearing?

'What do the Macbeths talk about when they've left the stage?'

'Probably what's for supper; but that's not Shakespeare's concern. There may be trivialities in their lives, but he is interested in their obsession. "Dramatic focus" is the applicable concept here.'

*****

'That idea about courses of action and inevitability. Fair enough. But isn't this a point in the play at which Macbeth could have escaped his fate? All he had to do was keep his imagination – about Banquo – under control.'

It's a bit late for that, the class decide. And in any case keeping his imagination under control is something Macbeth's not much good at. Furthermore, Banquo isn't the only threat Macbeth faces.

*****

Act Three Scene Three

Commentary

We were not witness to the murder of Duncan; but Shakespeare has decided to let us see Banquo being killed. Why?

> The sight of Macbeth, only just hailed as a hero, stabbing to death an old man in his bed might have been too much for the audience to bear, or at least believe. He is distanced from this second murder, however; and in addition our view of him has changed.
>
> More importantly for an Elizabethan audience, the first victim is a king, and watching him die would verge on the traumatic.

The third murderer is a mystery figure. Speculate about him if you wish; or ignore him, beyond acknowledging that if he has been sent by Macbeth to keep an eye on the other two that reinforces the theme of mistrust.

Don't worry either about the fact that the First Murderer speaks 'poetically': characters in poetic drama do, even when they're bad characters. Pay more attention perhaps to the fact that he speaks sensitively. Then accept that before he was *'tugged with fortune'* he may have been a very different man. (He has also retained a sense of humour, albeit grim – see *line 16*.)   *5-8*

They have been given a list of guests against which to check the arrivals: Macbeth being efficient. But they know Banquo anyway, and recognise him.   *9-11*

The striking out of the light? Symbolism? It helps Fleance escape, however: once again the minions are inefficient.   *15-20*

'Best half of our affair': this suggests that Fleance's death was more important to Macbeth than Banquo's. But Macbeth did not say that, so how did the Second Murderer pick it up? Perhaps more is known among the common people than Macbeth realises.

Overview: other things to note

Setting
o   The murder takes place at some distance from the palace but within its grounds. So it fulfils Macbeth's requirement that he maintain a *'clearness'* of the deed, while ensuring that the murderers do locate their victim. They are further assisted by the fact the Banquo and Fleance leave their horses (with grooms?) and walk the rest of the way.
o   The *'streaks of day'* noted by the First Murderer represent Banquo's last moments, and add intensity to his murder.

Character
o   The Third Murderer: let's speculate after all.
   •   Did Shakespeare initially intend that he should kill the other two on Macbeth's instructions? That's what we half-expect, and it would have been further proof of Macbeth's insecurity and ruthlessness.
   •   A few small changes would make him responsible for Fleance's escape, and we might then see him as having been sent by the Witches to ensure that their prophecies come true – he would be, in that scenario, the agents of the agents of darkness.
o   Banquo dies without any grand speeches, but nobly (he sends his son off to safety). The fact that it is so easy to

kill him and it happens so swiftly is in itself dramatically effective.

Action
o   The significance, for Macbeth, of Fleance's escape. This is a pivotal point in the action. From here on the Witches' other prophecies begin to come true.

Style
o   Realistic. We join the discussion in the middle (at *'But'*). It's tense, economical and fragmented, leaving plenty of room for as much action as a director wants to include.

Ideas
o   Mistrust
o   Fatherly care
o   Revenge

General
o   Main purpose: to prepare us for the banqueting scene

Student Response

'The ordinary people in the play are a pretty shabby lot. Not just the servants – Malcolm and Donalbain have run off without a fight, and everybody else seems to be letting Macbeth get away with what he has done.'

We talk about the difficulty of standing up to a tyrant. There are plenty of examples in the news. If one of Shakespeare's side-interests is the effect that people of power have on the lesser folk who live around them, then we might look for some pattern in how the minor characters respond to the events of the play.

'Minor characters in a play are often included simply because there are minor characters – people on the fringe of events – in real life.'

Can you give a better justification for the presence of the minor characters in the plays you have studied?

'Who are the minor characters?' We draw up a list. None of them is particularly interesting. Other Shakespeare plays have fascinating 'median' characters, i.e. important minor ones.

*****

Act Three Scene Four

Commentary

Staging this scene has always been a challenge: the movement of the actors must be carefully controlled and timed; and some early decisions need to be taken (e.g. will the ghost of Banquo actually appear on stage?)

Macbeth is playing the genial host; or maybe he *is* genial – he thinks his one remaining problem has been solved.   *2*

It's possible to detect some unease, however, in both him and his wife, in their new roles. They make a great show of ensuring that their guests feel welcome, and of not holding themselves aloof.   *3-8*

Shakespeare is very quick to introduce a further contrary element: the First Murderer enters almost immediately, and brings only partially good news. He has blood on his face (another sign of incompetence?) It is Banquo's blood, says the Murderer, and Macbeth's response is callous. *'Despatch'd'* – once more, an indirect term.   *14-15*

The Murderer is blunter, and proud of his work…but.   *16*

'The like': another off-hand phrase from Macbeth, who now seeks the added reassurance that news of Fleance's death will bring him.   *17-19*

He doesn't get it. The Murderers have not done their work well enough.   *20*

Why does Macbeth speak his next lines as an aside? He has nothing to hide from the Murderer – unless it is the fact that he is afraid. He is desperate for two things.   *21-25*
o   Security (the marble and rock images)   *22*
o   The freedom that security brings (the air image, and the references to different kinds of confinement. Macbeth does like to string words together!)   *23-24*

'Saucy' (unwelcome or intrusive) doubts and fears: just as the Murderer, with his ultimately bad news, is unwelcome at this feast.   *25*

'Safe': Macbeth once more uses a deliberately ambiguous term; but the irony rebounds on him when he comes to envy those (Duncan, Banquo) who now sleep safely, beyond his further reach.

The Murderer adds his own ironical meaning to *'safe'* (in line with the grim humour he showed during the murder itself); and *'bides'* means both 'lives' and 'stays'. His detailed account of Banquo's injuries makes clear the truth of the matter. Why does Shakespeare have him give those details?   *26*

---

o   To add to our sense of horror at what has been done
o   To prepare us for Banquo's return as a ghost: we will be able to recognise him instantly
o   To leave no doubt in our minds that he *is* dead

Dramatists do a lot of planning ahead (see later essay question, page 101).

Macbeth reassures himself that he will be safe until Fleance grows into an adult snake. But he wants to hear the details of the attack. *'We'll hear ourselves again'* probably means 'we (i.e. you and I, not the royal we) will hear ourselves talk about the murder again.' There is an implication that the Murderer   *29-31* *32* and he are together in this.

Lady Macbeth's role in this scene is that of an anchor to the world Macbeth and she have created and in which they hope to rule unchallenged. It is a world he keeps drifting away from as he thinks (here) about what has gone wrong, then has his visions; and she struggles to bring him back to it. *32-37*

Are her words spoken to Macbeth alone, or so that the whole company can hear them? She does not yet realise there is a problem and will see no need to take him aside (as later). This *sounds* like a gentle public reprimand.

'Sweet remembrancer': public or private? His next two lines, in which he continues her eating image, are certainly for general consumption. *37*

There's some doubt as to just when Shakespeare intended that the ghost should enter. Consider the different options yourself, and how this part of the scene might work.

Once again we find irony (like the evil acts of *Act One Scene Seven lines 7-10*) rebounding on the person who initiates it. Macbeth is fully aware of the hidden meaning of what he says here. He's covering his tracks, yes, but he's also secretly congratulating himself. Then his 'wish' comes true and Banquo appears. Here's something else about irony, then, at least as it would have been viewed by Shakespeare's audience: it represents a joke played on men by the forces which control their lives. *40-41*

'He's let us down,' Ross says. But in a more profound sense Banquo's *'promise'* as a leader will not, now, be fulfilled. *43-44*

The simplicity of the next few lines makes them starkly dramatic: such few words give rise to such massive upheaval. *46-50*

'Which of you have done this?': what two meanings can you see in this question?

> o   Who has murdered Banquo (whose dead body I now see before me)?
> o   Who has played this trick on me?

Which meaning would give greater insight into Macbeth's current state of mind?

The ghost cannot say he did it, Macbeth thinks, because....

> he didn't strike Banquo down himself: the blood is on the Murderer's face, not his.

'Gory locks': Make-up will ensure that the twenty gashes on Banquo's head identify him.

Lady Macbeth is quick to step into this disastrous moment in an attempt to control it. Look at the way her words in *line 53* parallel – answer – Ross's in the line before, phrase for phrase:

'Gentlemen'	-	*'worthy friends'*
'rise'	-	*'Sit'*
'his highness'	-	*'My lord'*
'is not'	-	*'is often'*

The very structure of the line offers reassurance.

But she has little comfort for Macbeth, only scorn: she falls back on a tried and trusted method of controlling him. *58*

And his response is predictable: he momentarily pulls himself together. *59-60*

His reply, however, is not good enough for her. *'O proper stuff'* (and nonsense) – scorn again. And she heaps on more. She seems to know what he has seen – another example of how well (at times) they can read each other's minds.

It was, she says, only an image (illusion) projected on his imagination by the actual thing he is afraid of. (Does she know what this is? Has he told her, as they prepared for the feast, what he arranged for Banquo? Or has she guessed?) *61*

He must have told her about the imaginary dagger, too, between times. If she realises he is seeing the ghost of Banquo sitting in his chair, that is also as far as she concerned only an *'air-drawn'* illusion. If she doesn't know what it is that has frightened him she's just saying, 'This looks like another one of your silly visions!'

More scorn is her answer in any case: this is a woman's fireside tale, shameful for a man to indulge in (sexual taunts again). More than that, *he* is *'shame itself'* – shame personified. The bluntness of her language is crushing: *'When all's done /You look but on a stool.'* *66* *67-68*

But she has lost him. He turns to the assembled gathering – surely they can see what he sees? He is virtually gibbering. He rebels against his own fear – *'Why, what care I?'* – but not for long. The ghost nods – perhaps an invitation for Macbeth to join it. But it will not speak. (There are three instances in the play when supernatural forces will not obey Macbeth's command to tell him more. We are only allowed to know, it seems, what will lead us a little further.) *69* *70*

There is no rest for us – not even for our bodies, in the ground. The carrion birds now become our friends: at least they will bury us permanently, after a fashion (in their stomachs). *71-73*

When the ghost disappears some brief normality returns. Part of that normality is that Lady Macbeth challenges his manhood, and he defends himself half-heartedly. *'If I stand here'*: perhaps he doubts that he does stand, with any security. (He sets great store by being solidly planted in the ground...but the ground, and he, both shake at times.) She seeks to shame him again.

'Blood hath been shed...': another disjointed speech from Macbeth, indicative of his distress. 'There's nothing new about murder; but it used to be that the dead would stay dead. Now they come alive again.' *75*

That's his speech in broad outline; but in passing he says some other interesting things. He implies that *'human statute'* – the rule of law – has led us into a happier time where murder is less common. What contribution can *he* think he has made to that civilising process? *76*

'Twenty mortal murders on their crowns': Banquo has twenty gashes on his head; but Macbeth is also thinking 'crown' as indicating head of family, and head of a family moreover that was destined to produce kings...and perhaps, now still is. *81*

'This is more strange /Than such a murder is': the unnatural consequences of an unnatural act are more surprising than the act itself, as if such actions are amplified in their effect. He may be thinking just about the appearance of the ghost; we may have in mind the fact that Macbeth, as the play progresses, *82-83*

is becoming more and more violent and acting more and more unnaturally (the 'course of action' concept again).

Lady Macbeth is still having difficulty. Does she speak *here* to Macbeth alone? *83-84*

Her words have some effect and he calms down. Does the audience suspect that this is only temporary? They certainly will when Macbeth wishes once more for Banquo's presence: that's an open invitation which we know the ghost will accept. (A horror-movie-maker's open secret – let the audience know that something terrible is going to happen just before it does.)

The ghost enters behind him – standard spookiness again. *91*

The ghost does not respond to him this time either: it is just *there*, and seems to bring no particular *93*
message. It is the sight of it alone that Macbeth cannot bear. It glares at him with eyes that have no
'speculation', i.e. cannot see; but an alternative meaning is 'understanding': Macbeth must fear that *95*
Banquo's ghost will know all his secrets.

Lady Macbeth is running out of excuses for him. *96-98*

Macbeth does not hear her attempts at a cover-up; his speech continues unbroken, and *'What man dare,* *99*
I dare' is addressed to the ghost (although it's something he has been driven to say to Lady Macbeth
twice, previously).

What's the purpose of the heroic images?

> To remind us that Macbeth is, or has been, heroic

'Firm...tremble': that concern with solidity again, and the fear of things which are unstable or *102-103*
insubstantial – witches that vanish into air, a ghost that is just a shadow or an *'unreal mockery'*...and *107*
promises that may turn out to be empty. These are the fears of a man of action and a soldier, one who,
when everything's reckoned up, was probably not cut out to be a king.

But the ghost seems to obey him. Another illusion?

Macbeth tells his guests to *'sit still'* ('carry on sitting' – they have begun to get up as if to leave). *108*
Things and people seated are for the moment stable, fixed in place. He needs that.

'Displaced...broke...disorder': the language of chaos. *109-110*

'Summer cloud': one that momentarily hides the sun; but Macbeth's sun has not shone recently, so that *111*
image is unrealistic; and he is exercised anyway by the question of what *is* real. His view of himself as
a brave man is challenged by the fact that he has gone pale with fear at the sight of the ghost, and his *112-116*
guests have not lost their colour at all.

But they have not seen the apparition. This is Macbeth's personal ghost, a manifestation of his own *116*
fear and guilt.

The best Lady Macbeth can do is get rid of everyone, without any ceremony – order is abandoned in *118-120*
the face of such disorder in Macbeth's behaviour.

Blood is mentioned four times in Macbeth's next speech. Favourite colours in set design and costume *122-126* for Macbeth? (No prizes.)

This is another fragmented speech betokening a fragmented mind. What is *'it'*?   *122*

o   Banquo's ghost?
o   Blood itself?

He shifts from one to the other, and includes Duncan's death as well as Banquo's.

'Blood will have blood': proverb – the way things are.   *122*

'Stones...move': instability. During Duncan's murder it was the stones that threatened to speak; just   *123*
before Macbeth's death it is the trees that move.

'Understood relations': the way things are (again), the patterns of existence which can be read in   *124*
prophetic signs – birds included – which can reveal a murderer no matter how well he hides.

'What is the night?': Macbeth struggles to return to the real world. But it is an indeterminate world,
neither night nor morning – symbolic of...

the uncertainty of Macbeth's fortunes at this point in the play.

In the real world there is the problem of Macduff to be dealt with. That too, is uncertain, however: *128-129*
Macbeth is not sure how Macduff stands, and asks his wife's advice. The consequences of his decision
not to share with her his plans for Banquo have shaken him.

Lady Macbeth suspects that once more Macbeth is fearing what may not need to be feared: she guesses   *129*
that he has not actually sent for Macduff so Macduff can not actually have 'denied' him.

She is right. But he *will* send for him, Macbeth says. This is true paranoia: if there is no evidence to   *130*
support your delusion, you create it. And you are insistent, as Macbeth is here: *'will...will...will...am*
bent...shall...shall'.

He does face one fact openly: that his own interests *('mine own good')* are more important to him than   *135*
anything else. He has never used the tyrant's subterfuge that what he has done, or is going to do, is
really for the sake of the country he tyrannises.

Macbeth's fortunes are in the balance; and he is at the midpoint in his 'course of [bloody] action'.   *136-138*
Everything can come together in the middle of a play, as well as at its end.

Macbeth still talks in ambiguities: the plans he has in his head (harm to Macduff, no doubt) need to be   *139-140*
carried out before they are *'scanned'* – but is that scanned by those around him, or by his own reason?
There is something of a blind forward rush in Macbeth's behaviour from now on. He has asked Lady
Macbeth's advice about Macduff but does not tell her what he has decided to do about him.

In acting contrary to natural law Macbeth has cut himself off from natural processes – like the   *141*
restorative one of sleep.

The only comfort Macbeth can offer is that they will soon become hardened to their own bloody   *142-144* cruelty. Lady Macbeth did want him to become pitiless, didn't she? She too, then, is getting (something of) her wish.

Overview: other things to note

Setting
- o   The kind of society Macbeth and his wife, as King and Queen, are seeking to establish. It's unlikely they would want it to be more egalitarian, despite the great show they make of mingling with their guests. But they seem to want it to be as sociable, and also as ceremonious, as Duncan's was. Their behaviour, though, is somewhat forced.
- o   The world beyond this

Character
- o   The last time Macbeth and Lady Macbeth appear together in the play. He now turns for help to the Witches instead of her.

Action
- o   The timing of the scene, halfway between night and day, and how that reflects the state of the action
- o   The last line of the scene points clearly forward.

Style
- o   The difficulty of conveying hysteria in words; hysteria is after all a denial of meaning.

Ideas
- o   Fear is in the eye of the beholder.

General
- o   The pathos of Macbeth's struggle to appear normal to his *'friends'*; and of Lady Macbeth's attempts to cover up for him; and the *'shame'* of their failure

Student Response

This scene was a lot of fun, all agree. That was partly because we acted it out.

> *'The theatre is a form of entertainment. If it does not entertain, it fails. If it entertains, it succeeds.'*

> *Show how the plays you have studied are designed to entertain.*

We discuss the elements in this scene that will entertain, unless the staging goes awry (which it can easily do, as we've just found). We've already talked about most of the other things the scene does.

*****

Then we list the things that 'come together' at this point in the play.

> *'In a well-made tragedy or comedy things come together, convincingly and with devastating or hilarious effect, at the end. They can come together in the middle of the play as well, however, and show us the way it is likely to go.'*

> *Discuss that statement in relation to plays you have studied.*

We know which way this play is likely to go because Macbeth himself tells us in no uncertain terms. 'It's like Shakespeare always wants us to know what's likely to happen next.'

Now might be a good time to tackle a (pretty straightforward) question about Macbeth and Lady Macbeth as a couple:

Show how the dramatists in plays you have studied explore the relationships between men and women, and discuss the means by which they make that exploration dramatically interesting.

The class agree it's pretty straightforward but choose not tackle it yet. 'We'll do it hereafter,' one of them says.

*****

Act Three Scene Five

Commentary

Let's assume Shakespeare wrote this scene (there's a lot of argument). Here are some questions about it.

o Why is Hecate angry?	*1*
o Is her description of Macbeth accurate?	*11-13*
o Make sure you know what the *'pit of Acheron'* is. That matters in the next scene.	*15*
o Is it Macbeth's end which she will be planning that night?	*20-21*
o *'Great business'* reminds us of	*22*
o The *'artificial'* sprites Macbeth will see the next day are unreal; but they are also full of 'artifice', meaning......	*27*
o What above all else will bring about Macbeth's downfall?	*32-33*
o Hecate is called away. What did we conclude when the Witches' familiars called them away in *Act One Scene One*?	*34-35*

---

o   Because *'the glory of their art'* has not been sufficiently demonstrated. She seems to feel that so far this has been a pretty miserable affair. (It's certainly been 'dour' to use a good Scots word – there have been few fireworks and little spectacle. She's also annoyed because she wasn't invited to take part – is there a touch of vanity (if not ambition) here?

o   Think about *'wayward'* (wilful) and *'son'* (whose son?)

o   A place in the lower depths of hell

o   Probably – she's taking over from the Witches (have they too proved themselves incompetent?)

o   *'This night's great business'*, Lady Macbeth's phrase *(Act One Scene Five line 66)*

o   Tricks

o   A false sense of security

o   That Shakespeare was emphasising how busy they were in their mischief. Same here.

Overview: other things to note

Setting
o   Vague, as usual for the Witches
o   The Witches too live in an ordered, 'ranked' society. Hecate reprimands them for being *'saucy'* (acting beyond their authority) and they are careful not to upset her further *(line 36)*.

Character
o   Hecate has some human characteristics...

Action
o   Just an atmospheric pause

Style
o   Its comparative simplicity. Is life less complicated for the powers of darkness, who need to see things from only one angle?

Ideas
o   Social order: necessary to all creatures
o   Deceitfulness (particularly of feelings of safety...remember the irony of reversal)

o   It's easy to see why this scene is often dropped from performances.

Student Response

'Hecate reminds me of someone I know!'

'Do any of you know anybody like Macbeth? Or Lady Macbeth?'

'I know somebody like the Porter.'

But the class all feel they now 'know' Macbeth and Lady Macbeth themselves; and we talk about how drama extends (and deepens) our knowledge and experience, and enables us to lead lives beyond our own.

*****

Act Three Scene Six

Commentary

Shakespeare lets us know that the forces against Macbeth are beginning to build.

We come in once more in the middle of a discussion. What impression does that give here?

> Fears about Macbeth have been growing and may already have been voiced, even in an indirect way (as now)

It is not only the forces (elsewhere) but the suspicions nearer to home that are stirring.

Lenox's speech is a masterpiece of duality. Read it aloud, twice...
o   as if you are loyal subject of Macbeth's who believes he is an honourable man who has acted in Scotland's best interests, and
o   as if you think he is a vicious murderer but dare not say so...and your speech is designed to sound out the Lord's feelings about him.

What differences do you notice in the way you speak in each case?

> *'Strangely' (line 3)* is the key word, really: you'll have found yourself speaking strangely the second time around, dropping your voice at times, pausing at others, emphasising the ironical bits (the ones with an intended meaning opposite to the superficial one).

Lenox is careful: *'only, I say'* means, 'All I'm saying is,' or, 'Don't get me wrong, but…'   **2**

He simply points to the disparity between the innocent things Duncan and Banquo did (Duncan was gracious, and allowed himself to be pitied by Macbeth – doesn't quite make sense of course – and Banquo was out walking after dark) and the terrible things that happened to them.   **3-5**

He seems to be agreeing with the suggestion that Malcolm and Donalbain killed their father, since they ran away. By the same token, he says, Fleance should be blamed for Banquo's death, since he ran away too.   **6-7**

But there were such obvious reasons why all three sons should want to depart quickly that the evidence and therefore the conclusion in both cases is revealed as absurd – without Lenox having to say that. The parallel does it for him.

'Men must not walk too late' (another hidden concern stated as a piece of sound advice): there's something sadly wrong when a man can't go out safely after sunset.   **7**

Note the weight of Lenox's rhetorical questions, and of his (ironical) exclamations *(lines 10-11)*.   **8-14**

'Delinquents' means both 'depraved men' and 'men who were delinquent in their duty' – i.e. did their job badly (where have we heard that before?)

'So that, I say': 'So my conclusion is that.'   **16**

But it's an ambiguous conclusion. What does *'borne all things well'* mean? 'Borne all things well for mine own good' Macbeth would now say. *17*

Did you find yourself adopting a mock-threatening tone when you read *lines 17-20* for the second time? That was you pretending, with Lenox, to be a supporter of public justice, while questioning, underneath all of that, just what sort of justice would be meted out to the fugitives if they were caught.

Which of the following does *'But, peace!'* mean? *21*
o 'Don't tell anybody what I've said.'
o 'Let's not worry any more for the moment.'

Macduff is in more immediate danger, and Lenox wants to know where he is. *21-24*

Why, however, does he now call Macbeth a *'tyrant'* openly?
o He has become confident, and now believes he can trust the Lord not to betray him.
o They have been playing a game all the time – having fun together at Macbeth's expense if you like. That's a more adventurous interpretation, but it would allow us to take *'But, peace!'* as meaning, 'Okay, let's talk more directly now.'

Why does Lenox ask where Macduff is, do you think?

o So that we learn that Macduff has gone to England and has met up with Malcolm, and they will be working against Macbeth o So that we know that other Scottish Lords (Lenox himself, here) are reviewing their allegiance to Macbeth

The Lord responds in kind: Macbeth is a tyrant also, as far as he is concerned. The *'malevolence'* which has driven Malcolm to England is ascribed to *'fortune'*; but Macbeth is clearly the medium through which that fortune has operated. *25* *28*

Then comes an account of the forces ranged against Macbeth. They include the *'holy'* king, and God. *29*

Macbeth has not been the only one to suffer sleepless nights. The effect of the tragic hero's behaviour on those around him (particularly when he falls) is a common focus of interest in tragedy. It is a quiet life they all seek. Macbeth too, now...but too late. It is also an ordered one, with homage paid 'faithfully' to those to whom it is rightfully owed; and it is one in which *'free'* honours are received, i.e. honours which can be accepted free of any strings. *34-36*

Macbeth has done what he said he was going to do: he has sent for Macduff (to call him to Court, presumably). Macduff rebuffed the messenger, who went off in a Machuff (sorry, too much to resist). *40-43*

Lenox reinforces his earlier *'tyrant'* with *'hand accursed!'* Macbeth has become the *'man forbid'* of *Act One Scene Three line 21.*

Overview: other things to note

<u>Setting</u>
o *Very* vague.
o The various worlds of the play:
   • the unrighteous one Macbeth, on the face of it, controls
   • the God-supported world of the English court

- this one, which could go either way
- the 'other world' controlled by the powers of darkness, which we and Macbeth are about to visit once more

Character
o   Depends whether we think Lenox and the Lord share a sense of bitter humour.

Action
o   Change in Macbeth's fortunes. He is soon to be a hunted man.

Style
o   Contrast between the calmness of the style in this whole scene and the swings and intensity of most other scenes in the play. How does this aspect of the scene's style assist Shakespeare in his purpose?

> It emphasises that the forces ranged against Macbeth are cautious, measured, inexorable.

o   The religious references. Good and bad men are clearly divided.

Ideas
o   Ultimate Justice

General
o   One of those necessary but dull scenes

Student Response

'Can we read about the Witches now please?'

'Not till we've talked about dramatic pace.'

So we talk about it, and the class are left with an essay:

'Changes of pace and mood should support rather than interrupt the audience's involvement with a play.'

Discuss this comment in relation to plays you have studied.

*****

Additional questions (A Level)

1. Show how in Act Three the balance of events begins to tip against Macbeth.

2. 'The plain speaking in this act is as dramatically effective as the high poetry.' Discuss

Commentary practice

This time the words, phrases and lines which could be used to answer each question have been underlined. Your job is to write the notes. Then if you're preparing for an A Level exam you may choose to write the whole commentary. IB candidates can deliver the commentary (into a tape recorder?)

Practice Commentary 3

Sample passage

BANQUO: To be thus, is nothing,

        But to be safely thus – Our fears in Banquo

        Stick deep, and in his royalty of nature

        Reigns that which would be fear'd; 'tis much he dares;

        And, to that dauntless temper of his mind,   *5*

        He hath a wisdom that doth guide his valour,

        To act in safety. There is none but he

        Whose being I do fear: and under him,

        My genius is rebuk'd, as, it is said,

        Mark Antony's was by Caesar. He chid the sisters,   *10*

        When first they put the name of king upon me,

        And bade them speak to him; then, prophet-like,

        They hailed him father to a line of kings.

        Upon my head they placed a fruitless crown,

        And put a barren sceptre in my gripe,   *15*

        Thence to be wrenched with an unlineal hand,

        No son of mine succeeding. If't be so,

        For Banquo's issue have I filed my mind;

        For them the gracious Duncan have I murdered;

        Put rancours in the vessel of my peace   *20*

        Only for them, and mine eternal jewel

        Given to the common enemy of man,

        To make them kings, the seeds of Banquo kings!

        Rather than so, come, fate into the list,

        And champion me to th' utterance! – Who's there?   *25*

Guiding questions

  a) What do we learn from this passage about Macbeth's attitude towards Banquo?

  b) How does Macbeth's style of speech reflect his state of mind?

Act Four

Act Four Scene One

Commentary

We shouldn't underestimate the power of this scene – to entertain, yes, but also to add more texture to some of the play's themes, and to its mood.

Macbeth has been driven, by what he saw at his own banquet, to visit the Witches in *their* kitchen, where they are preparing a feast for his eyes (this is of course a very visual scene).

Just how fully the details of the scene add to the atmosphere of the play at this point will become apparent if you complete the following table, which lists the items the witches throw into the cauldron. For each item tick the box(es) which indicate the theme(s) to which it contributes.

Item	Poison	Night, darkness, blindness	Cutting, dismemberment	Eating, greed, lustfulness	Unnatural-ness, irreligion
Entrails					
Toad					
Snake fillet					
Newt's eye					
Frog's toe					
Bat's wool					
Dog's tongue					
Adder's fork					
Blind-worm's sting					
Lizard's leg					
Owl's wing					
Dragon's scale					
Wolf's tooth					
Witches' mummy					
Shark's stomach					
Hemlock root					
Jew's liver					
Goat's gall					
Slips of yew					
Turk's nose					
Tartar's lips					
Baby's finger					
Tiger's stomach					
Baboon's blood					
Sow's blood					
Gibbet grease					

On the next page you will find a completed table for comparison.

Item	Poison	Night, darkness, blindness	Cutting, dismemberment	Eating, greed, lustfulness	Unnatural-ness, irreligion
Entrails	x		x		
Toad	x	x			
Snake fillet	x		x		
Newt's eye		x	x		
Frog's toe			x		
Bat's wool		x			
Dog's tongue			x		
Adder's fork	x		x		
Blind-worm's sting	x	x	x		
Lizard's leg			x		
Owl's wing		x	x		
Dragon's scale					x
Wolf's tooth				x	
Witches' mummy					x
Shark's stomach			x	x	
Hemlock root	x	x			
Jew's liver			x		x
Goat's gall			x	x	
Slips of yew	x	x	x		x
Turk's nose			x		x
Tartar's lips			x		x
Baby's finger			x		x
Tiger's stomach			x	x	
Baboon's blood			x	x	
Sow's blood			x		x
Gibbet grease					x

What do you notice about the items associated with greed and unnaturalness, i.e. the ones most closely linked with Macbeth's behaviour?

> They are clustered in the second half of the list: as the potion is created, it takes on a more pointed reference to Macbeth, who is about to enter.

Why do you think the theme of cutting, separating, has prominence in the list?

> People are being separated from each other; the country is divided; Macbeth and his wife have parted company and Macbeth is increasingly isolated.

Other parts of the opening dialogue will probably have reminded you of details from earlier in the play.
o   *'Thrice'*   *1*
o   *'Tis time'*   *3*
o   *'Double, double'*   *10*
o   *'Fillet...fenny; boil...bake'*   *12-13*
o   *'gruel thick and slab'*   *32*

Two other details, examples of powerful poetic sound-effects.
o   *'cold stone' (line 6)*: the long, hollow vowel sounds
o   *'Open locks /Whoever knocks (46-47)'*: short and dramatic lines announcing Macbeth's arrival

Macbeth is not cowed by the Witches: the rhythm and diction of his opening lines are aggressive. (See the discussion of his whole demeanour in this scene under Character, below.)   *48-49*

'A deed without a name': None of the evil acts in the plays is named directly. Remember Macbeth's and Lady Macbeth's reluctance to speak straightforwardly of Duncan's murder. Think also about the age-old idea (remember Rumpelstiltskin) that by knowing and using the name of something you have power over it. Macbeth does not name his actions for what they are; and he has no power over them.

The gist of Macbeth's next speech is not altogether clear. If you try to summarise it you'll find there's   *50*
no certain main idea. He seems to be asking the Witches (commanding? – it depends on the weight you give to the word *'conjure'*) to tell him what he asks. But is he referring to the questions he will try (and fail) to get answers to from the apparitions? Or is he referring back to *'What is't you do?' (line 49)*? If it's the latter, then that question may mean much more than 'What are you doing here?' Suggest an alternative.

It's the word *'though'* which is principally puzzling. Here are two alternative readings of the speech.
o   'Even though you are so powerful that you can control the winds etc, I command you to tell me…'
o   'Even though what you tell me may be news of the imminent destruction of the world, I command you to speak.'

A further interpretation, favoured by some commentators, is
o   'Even though what I am doing may bring about the end of the world, I am determined to press on.'
This reading is not really borne out by the literal meaning of the words; but it is very much in line with Macbeth's increasing recklessness (remember *'let the frame of things disjoint, both the worlds suffer,/Ere we will eat our meat in fear' Act Three Scene Three lines 16-17*). It is moreover what the audience may *hear* in the lines. ('As often in drama, it's the impression, not the facts, which matters.')

Details of the speech you may wish to note:

'Fight /Against the churches': the Witches as instruments of the world's dark – here anti-Christ –   *52-53*
forces.

'Confound…navigation': both *'sink…ships'* and *'confuse…navigators'*. Discuss which one is more   *54*
appropriate to Macbeth's situation and more closely linked to the play's themes.

The images of things being levelled (laid low). You may want to go into detail: if Macbeth himself is one of the things which will in the end be brought down, remember that Duncan 'planted' him; *'trees'* will help topple him; and the battlements of Macbeth's own castle threatened Duncan.   *55*

The idea of a castle falling on the head of its guardian and killing him? Ironical in so far as the castle was supposed to give him protection; and a reminder of Macbeth's failure as a king in that he was supposed to be the *'warder'* of the country's well-being.   *56*

'Germen': a very fundamental concept – the essential element of Creation. Macbeth acknowledges its value (*'treasure'*) but is prepared, perhaps, to see it fall into disorder in order to preserve his own power (and perhaps, too, does not see the illogicality of that).   *59*

'Even till destruction sicken': he foreshadows his own ultimate feelings of abhorrence at the bloody havoc he will cause.   *60*

The *'armed* (helmeted) *head'* is commonly taken to represent Macbeth, in which case he is questioning and answering himself. That explains *'He knows thy thought'* and gives rise to the conjecture that in this as in other scenes involving apparitions Macbeth is imagining the whole thing.   *68*

The Second Apparition, *'a bloody child'*, is clearly Macduff shortly after his arrival in the world (by Caesarean operation, so that he was in that sense not *'of woman born'*).   *76*

'Had I three ears': see discussion under <u>Character</u>.   *78*

'Then live, Macduff: what need I fear of thee?': but he tries to kill him anyway. Much of the violence Macbeth commits is pointless, and not only because it is never more than partially effective.   *82*

It's not altogether clear how Macbeth is going to take out a *'bond of fate'* in killing Macduff. Is he hoping to buy, by this bloody act, a promise from fate that he will be safe? He has already had one promise, that he can not be harmed by one of woman born, so this will be his second, *'double'* assurance. He will use the bond to prove Fear a liar and to make it possible to sleep…at last.   *84*

The Third Apparition is Malcolm, who will trick Macbeth by making Birnam Wood a moveable forest. The apparition itself seeks to deceive him more fundamentally here by reassuring him that all is well.   *86*
90-94

He is for the moment convinced. The temporary respite from anxiety he has gained is reflected in the simple certainty of *'That will never be'* and the buoyancy of the rhetorical question, exclamations and command which follow.   *94*
96-100

Who are the *'Rebellious dead' (line 97)*?

> Predominantly Banquo, but perhaps Duncan also…and maybe Macduff (whom he is yet to kill); and beyond that all who have died under his rule (are there some we have not heard about?)

What's the effect of *'rise…rise' (lines 97-98)*?

> Some editors have argued that the second *'rise'* is an early copyist's error; but the repetition emphasises the antithesis in the two lines, which is in turn a mark of Macbeth's new-found confidence.

'Our high-placed Macbeth' (line 98): see the discussion under <u>Character</u>.

'Shall live the lease of nature' (will live a normal life-span): is he now willing to settle for an unhappy life provided it doesn't come to a premature end? (Note the legal terminology: it has all become for Macbeth a matter of doing the best deal he can.)

But seeing *'Banquo's issue'* ascend to the throne would make it *too* unhappy, and the question of whether they will now becomes the most important one of all for him.   *100-103*

'I will be satisfied': peremptory verging on petty. Othello uses almost the same words when he seeks proof of Desdemona's infidelity. Is there jealousy in Macbeth also?   *104*

The eight kings are to come, and leave, *'like shadows'*. But before they go they will have destroyed for ever Macbeth's peace of mind.   *111*

Macbeth was on fire for the kingship; the sight of the crown on the head of the first king, obviously a descendant of Banquo, burns his eyes.   *113*

Note how questions, exclamations, dashes and generally broken syntax indicate Macbeth's distress. (Popular Guiding Question: 'How does ....'s style of speech reflect his or her state of mind?')   *115-124*

'Th' crack of doom' (line 117): The Day of Judgement, i.e. the end of time, rather than Macbeth's own day of judgement, which will come much earlier.

The next passage is little more than an excuse for a bit of spectacle (and perhaps paid a compliment to King James when he was in the audience); but it does also prepare us for the Witches' exit, and lightly mocks Macbeth, maybe in response to whatever lack of respect he showed to the Witches earlier in the scene (see, again, discussion under <u>Character</u>).

Why did Macbeth not come here alone?

Why has Lenox stayed with him in spite of the doubts he expressed in *Act Three Scene Six*?

Why did the Witches not allow Lenox to see them? (They let Banquo.)   *136-137*

'Damned all those that trust them': Does Macbeth include himself? It's ironical either way.   *139*

The sound of hooves: almost as ominous as the knocking on the gate. He no longer expects good news.   *140*

A problem for the actor playing Lenox: what does he do while Macbeth speaks his aside?

Macbeth's language immediately after the departure of the Witches has been very functional,   *144-146*
colloquial almost. He now moves awkwardly into philosophising vein: the first line of his speech splutters; the next two, it has been pointed out, are not strictly logical (although the general meaning is plain enough).

'Firstlings' suggests 'first-born', ideas which he will father in his imagination. The incongruity between the innocence of newly-born infants and the terrible plans he now engenders adds a sense of horror to the lines.

The antitheses – *'heart...hand; thoughts...acts; thought...done'* – emphasise his determination. The   *147-149*
string of violent alliterative words – *'surprise...seize...give to the edge o' the sword'* – indicate   *149-150*
something of his haste.

Why does he plan to kill Macduff's offspring? It's not as if the Witches have indicated that they pose

any danger to Macbeth's kingship. Is this pure retribution, nastiness? Why, then, the phrase *'unfortunate souls'*, as if he feels some sympathy towards his intended victims? Perhaps this threatens   *151*
the onset of the kind of internal debate we have seen him conduct at earlier points in the action, and he
immediately suppresses it with a firm rhyming couplet.   *153-154*

'But no more sights!': dramatically powerful, allowing the actor to reveal the turmoil beneath the   *155*
determination…which is resumed in the final lines of the scene.

Overview: other things to note

Setting
o   Inside, somewhere *('knocks', 'locks', 'come in')*; but this is also *'the pit of Acheron'*, a part of Hell. Macbeth is, as we say, 'looking into the depths'.
o   There is a hierarchy in the Witches' world too *('our masters…Come high or low')*.
o   Thunder: occurs at the beginning of the scene and with the appearance of each of the first three apparitions. It is a symbol not only of the power of the Witches and the forces controlling them but of the disturbed state of Macbeth's mind – he must learn to sleep *'in spite of'* it.
o   The historical context (well-known to Shakespeare's audience) – e.g. the 'show of Kings'. Does a modern audience's comparative lack of historical knowledge hinder its understanding, or enjoyment, of the play?

Character
o   Macbeth: there is scope for reading into his words in this scene some of the grim humour we thought he might have demonstrated when we heard how he despatched Macdonwald *(Act One Scene Two lines 21-23)* and in his reference to his three ears in *line 78*. That would help explain some of the things he says here which have given commentators difficulty, as well as some elements in his *style* of speech…

Imagine yourself playing the part of Macbeth in this scene with an ironical smile on your lips as you speak, and even a glint in your eye.
   • Your first words *(lines 48-49)* are informal, challenging, brusque almost: you are trying to show the Witches that you are not afraid of them.
   • You cast some doubt on their authority to speak *('by that which you profess, /Howe'er you come to know it', lines 50-51)*.
   • *'Call 'em; let me see 'em' (line 63)*: rough, 'I'll take no nonsense from you or your masters' tone
   • *'Whate'er thou art' (line 73)*: close to scathing
   • *'Had I three ears' (line 78)*: as near to joking as you come anywhere in the play
   • *'laugh to scorn' (Second Apparition, line 79)*: is this prompted by the fact that you are already (after a fashion) laughing?
   • *'sleep in spite of thunder (line 86)'*: an ironical reference, perhaps accompanied by a gesture, to what is going on in the background? The latest peal of thunder could be timed to match your words.
   • You take over the rhyming couplets of the Witches as if you are mocking them *(lines 94-102)*.
   • *'Sweet bodements! Good!' (line 96)*: almost cheery
   • *'our high-placed Macbeth' (line 98)*: one of the phrases which has puzzled commentators. It now takes on a tongue-in-cheek aspect – are you poking wry fun at yourself?
   • *'if your art can tell so much' (lines 101-102)*: sarcastic again?
   • *'And an eternal curse fall on you' (line 105)*: you must surely be aware of the irony in the fact that you are threatening those who have the power to place a curse on *you*. (You do a lot of cursing in this scene.)

So there's a case to be made for a slightly different Macbeth from the harried, haunted and unhappy figure he usually appears to be. His dour amusement (if it *is* that) humanises him. Note, however, that he doesn't find the show of Kings at all funny: it carries too bleak a message. Whatever grim humour he has shown now gives way to pure grimness; and it is the turn of the Witches to jest at his expense *('but why/Stands Macbeth thus amazedly?' lines 125-126).*

Action
o   Begins a new phase in the narrative, just as the Witches' earlier scenes did.

Style
o   The use of short lines and rhyme (Witches and Apparitions) to demarcate the two worlds; and Macbeth's brief crossing of the boundary in *lines 94-101*

Ideas
o   Appearance and reality (in a variety of ways)
o   Reward (and punishment): *'every one shall share i' th' gains' (line 40)*
o   The doubling of things: the witches double their power through magic; Macbeth plans to double his safety by killing Macduff even though there is no need to. The unnatural consequences of an unnatural act are magnified, as we noted earlier.

General
o   Do we expect to see the Witches again later in the play?

Student Response

'Aren't the Apparitions working against each other? The first one frightens Macbeth; the second and third try to trick him into a false sense of security which will contribute to his downfall; then the show of Kings gets in the way of that.'

'Perhaps part of the Witches' overall strategy is to confuse Macbeth so that he does not know who or what to believe.'

*****

'How does an actor know whether Shakespeare intended Macbeth to show a sense of humour?'

'He doesn't. It's a matter of professional judgement, of "feel for the text" if you like.' We return to the earlier essay question:

> *'When we are not exactly sure what the words or the events of a play mean, we should see that as an opportunity rather than a problem.'*
>
> *What opportunities for interpretation have you found in the texts of your chosen plays? How can that freedom strengthen rather than weaken a play's impact?*

It's not just the audience, or the reader, who has some freedom of interpretation, but the director and actors also. That's one of the things which makes going to the theatre enjoyable – you never quite know how a play is going to be presented on stage. In this particular instance an actor, or director, may decide that lightening Macbeth's character (slightly) will deepen the sense of tragedy when he falls. There's no comedy as such in the play (the Porter's monologue hardly qualifies as an instance of comic relief) but if we substitute 'humour' for 'comedy' in the following question –

> *'Show how dramatists can use comedy to increase the impact of tragedy'* –

we might just be able to use Macbeth's words in this scene and the Porter's in *Act Two* to put together a brief answer.

*****

Act Four Scene Two

Commentary

Lady Macduff can not see beyond the injustice of the situation to its practicalities. A man should only flee when he has done something bad, she says. Macduff has done nothing bad so should not have run away. In fact his flight was in itself bad, since he has left his family exposed.

1

The question, 'What is a traitor?' runs through the scene. Lady Macduff does not believe her husband is a traitor to Macbeth (his *'actions'* have done nothing to suggest that); but he has been a traitor to himself and his family in allowing his fears to overcome his protective instincts.

3

4

Ross argues that fleeing might have been the wise thing to do (and we know that he is right – Macbeth has already moved against Macduff).

4-5

But leaving his family unprotected was unnatural, Lady Macduff says, particularly when he acted through fear for his own safety. Note the bird image and compare it with the *'mousing owl'* of *Act Two Scene Four lines 12-13*. Her attack on her husband is measured as well as bitter: look at the shape of her final sentence, a triangle marked out by *'All...nothing...little'* and underlined by the alliteration of the last line.

9-12

12-14

Macduff is presented here as a worthy opponent *('noble, wise, judicious')* for Macbeth (see discussion under Action below).

16

'The fits o' the season': 'The way things are now' (compare *'the times'* in the next line, and Lady Macbeth's *'look like the time'*, *Act One Scene Five line 62*, which we suggested might mean 'follow the current fashion'). A more precise meaning might be 'the uncertainties of life at the moment', with a side reference in *'fits'* towards Macbeth's violent outbursts.

17

Ross adds to our understanding of what it can mean to be a traitor.
o   In times like these, since our loyalties are divided, we must betray one side or the other, and may not realise it. We can therefore be unwitting traitors.
o   In acting as traitors we *'do not know'* (i.e. turn our backs on, deny) *ourselves'*.

18-19

(For a discussion of whether Ross himself may be a traitor in a more horrific sense see under Character.)

He then takes an ambiguous path in his attempts to reassure Lady Macduff. He blames on the *'cruel* (and uncertain) *times'* the fact that we are driven to act on rumour since we can have no sure knowledge of *'what we fear'*. He seems here to be justifying, once more, Macduff's flight – he was wise to run away since rumour (and there must have been lots of that about Macbeth's behaviour) was all he had to go on. Ross may also, however, be counselling Lady Macduff against judging her husband's behaviour on inadequate knowledge of (rumour about) his reasons.

20

He is struggling with his own feelings, however; and his sense of confusion and powerlessness is summed up in the sea image.

21-22

'Move': your edition may read *'none'*. The general sense does not change, however. *'Move'* would mean that the sentence is unfinished, a sign of Ross's distress. *'None'* would carry the idea that we wash backwards and forwards but in no overall direction.

'Shall not be long...again': see discussion under Character.

23

His final reassurance is weak; but maybe that's what the situation demands. *24-25*

'*My pretty cousin*': paves the way for the pathos which follows.

'*Fathered...fatherless*': Lady Macduff's paradox labours the point somewhat; and the rest of the scene is laboured, too. *27*

Ross leaves in order to avoid weeping (he says). *28-30*

The term most often used to describe Macduff's son as he appears in the remainder of the scene is 'precocious' (too smart for his years). That's an effect aimed at by Shakespeare, however. His very chirpiness adds to the pathos of the scene, and increases our sense (important to tragedy) that something of value (here, a bright and brave little soul) is about to be lost. His mother is used largely to show him off: he is always one step ahead of her in the discussion, and she feeds him some useful lines.

That's not the only artifice in the dialogue: the '*worms and flies*' image looks forward to his death. *33*

What kind of '*bird*' is he, do you think? *35*

> A wren, diminutive but courageous, as his mother thinks his father should have been?

The bird-traps all work by deceit. *35-36*

'*Not dead...Yes, he is dead*': she must mean 'dead to all intents and purposes, since he soon will be.' But why, since he has escaped? Shakespeare is more concerned to keep the banter going. Is Lady Macduff indulging her son? Is there a wry smile on her lips? Is there just a touch of (sad) humour in this interchange, and is it designed to provide something *approaching* comic relief? Even a little smile at a time like this can help an audience face up to what will follow...and can also shock by contrast. *38-39*

'*What is a traitor?*': the question again. Lady Macduff's answer is direct; but who is she referring to? *47-48*

> o   All men who speak dishonestly
> o   Macduff, who has sworn a marriage vow and now betrayed it

Does she regard Macduff as a traitor both generally and in respect to her?

> No: she does not believe he has acted traitorously towards Macbeth *(lines 1,3)*.

'*Then the liars...hang up them*': the logic of 'the innocent eye'. Note the pert rhythm of the last three words. *55-56*

It's been claimed that if you give six chimpanzees a typewriter each and leave them long enough they'll come up with the Complete Works of Shakespeare. That says much more about the laws of probability than about the quality of Shakespeare's plays; but this particular '*poor monkey*' has delivered one truth at least, randomly or not. *57*

'But how wilt thou do for a father?': yes, this *is* laboured – there's no call for her to return to the   *59-60*
painful question. But it's the one uppermost in her mind, and it both underlines her anguish and allows
more significant – and cynical – prattle.

The Messenger reinforces the impression left by Ross: that everyone in Scotland is now in fear of his
or her life. He also adds to the suspense of this part of the scene, by his three references to the
imminence of what is to happen. The three are?

o	*'nearly'*
o	*'nigh'*
o	*'no longer'*

He contributes to the pathos, too. In what phrases?

o	*'your state of honour'*
o	*'a homely man's advice'*
o	*'your little ones'*
o	*'Heaven preserve you!'*
(Loss, simplicity, innocence, righteousness)	

'Whither' (*'Whether'* in some editions) would make more sense if it was 'Wherefore' ('Why'), since   *70*
she is protesting that she has no reason to fly...until she realises (she has caught cynicism from her son,
it seems) that the world's values have been turned on their head in these troubled times. It is no longer
enough to be innocent.

'Where is thy husband?': the Murderer's question is unnecessary. But then so is the violence.   *77*

A reminder that Macduff is in a 'sanctified' place at the English Court, from where he will sally out   *78-79*
against Macbeth. Lady Macduff's demeanour in these lines?

'Traitor': the simplest sense of the word, even if not accurate.   *79*

'Shag-eared villain': whatever its precise meaning, the phrase suggests that Macbeth has had to scrape   *80*
the bottom of the barrel to find men willing to do his dirty work for him.

'Egg...fry' (no pun intended, surely!): the innocence of the very young; and a reminder that *'issue'* is
what's at issue, at least in Macbeth's mind.

The little boy's protectiveness toward his mother echoes, pitifully, hers towards him and Banquo's   *82*
towards Fleance in similar circumstances.

Why are we allowed to see *this* murder on stage?

Overview: other things to note

Setting
o   Somebody else's castle. Macbeth is reaching out into the community.
o   Scotland in turmoil. The whole of society is threatened: the Messenger is an ordinary man.

Character
o   Lady Macduff: shows herself to almost as capable of scorn as Lady Macbeth. She acts as a contrast to Lady Macbeth, throwing into relief, by her protectiveness of her family, Lady Macbeth's lack of motherly feeling.
o   Ross: presented here as a 'good' man; but he, too, flees. What about the suggestion that he is in fact one of the Murderers sent by Macbeth, and returns *('Shall not be long but I'll be here again')* to assist in the killing? He has perhaps come on ahead to warn Lady Macduff, and becomes, if that is the case, another example of a man torn in his loyalties, or struggling between fear (of the tyrant) and sympathy (for his victims). Look again at his sea image *(lines 21-22)*.

Action
o   Prepares for Macduff's confrontation with Macbeth. Essay question:

'Dramatists must plan ahead.'

What examples have you found in the plays you have studied of dramatists planning ahead?

o   Variation in pace: the scene is leisurely to begin with, then speeds up in the middle.

Style
o   The banter between Lady Macduff and her son is in prose, like the Porter's speech and most clowning in Elizabethan drama.
o   The amount of blessing in this scene almost matches the amount of cursing Macbeth did in the previous one – the polarities of good and evil reflected in language.

Ideas
o   Ambition: dangerous (traps are not set for *'poor birds', line 37*)
o   The prerequisites of an ordered society. The Law must be accepted by all, even those who break it (remember the manner of Cawdor's death – *'very frankly he confessed his treasons'*). If the liars and swearers deny the Rule of Law and turn on the honest men, then the very structure of society is destroyed and chaos reigns. Macbeth the liar and swearer has turned against Duncan the honest man, and brought havoc on Scotland.
o   Courage in the face of death (Cawdor; here, Lady Macduff; at the end of the play, Young Siward then Macbeth)

General
o   The cruelty of it – evidence of Macbeth's continued slide

Student Response

'What does *laboured* mean?'

'Showing signs that it is spoken (by the character) or written (by the dramatist) with difficulty.' (My explanation.)

'So it can also be hard work for the audience. This scene is unconvincing.'

'Wait till you read the next one.' (My warning.)

*****

'The scene doesn't make sense! Why has Macbeth killed Macduff's family? He's only caused trouble for himself.'

We decide there has been no logic in what Macbeth has caused to happen here, no rational explanation for his behaviour, that is. But we remind ourselves that he has gone beyond reason, that a man afraid (and frustrated, and haunted by visions) does not have to act rationally in order to appear convincing on stage. Quite the opposite.

But there's another kind of logic in operation, also:

> *'There is such a thing as dramatic logic, and it is a necessary component of any good play: without it the play will neither convince the audience nor hold together on the stage.'*

> *Discuss the dramatic logic of the plays you have studied.*

We discuss the dramatic logic of the scene. These events are part of the pattern of existence Shakespeare is making plain to his audience – the following of a course of action leading from virtue to damnation. It is the logic of The Fall. It is the logic of gravity. Dramatic logic, which must follow the Laws of Creation, overrides human logic.

*****

Act Four Scene Three

Commentary

It sounds to begin with as if Malcolm has given up; but this is part of his testing of Macduff.	*1-2*
Note Macduff's heroic image, in contrast: they should stand over their fallen country and defend her.	*3-5*
His speech is prophetic: he is a new widower.	*5*
Heaven personified, as throughout the scene: it has been, earlier, a feeling observer of events, is now a suffering victim, and will become a participant in the action.	*6-8*

Malcolm again plays the cautious man, who will not move against Macbeth until he has more proof and greater support, and the time is right. He probes Macduff by pretending to doubt him, on the following grounds. *8-11*
o   Macduff may turn out to be as deceitful as Macbeth, who *'Was once thought honest'*.
o   Macduff was once loyal to Macbeth, and may be so still.
o   Macbeth has not harmed Macduff – that's suspicious.
o   Macduff could gain favour from Macbeth by tricking Malcolm into returning to Scotland.

Images to note…
o   *'Blisters' (line 12)*: what poison does to the tongue
o   Sacrifice *(lines 16-17)*: the weak Malcolm and the all-powerful Macbeth – part of Malcolm's pretence?

'Wail…will…well' (lines 8,10,13): any connection other than that of sound?

> *'wail'*: inactive suffering
> *'will'*: determination to act
> *'well'*: doubts about Macduff's trustworthiness, which hold him back

'I am not treacherous': if you were playing Macduff, how would you speak the line?	*18*
Malcolm then gives Macduff a chance to confess without wholly damning himself…'You may *not* be a traitor: you could just be a good man who against his will has been corrupted by *Macbeth's* treachery and driven back (forced to *'recoil'*) by the power of his *'charge'* (as in the backwards blast from a cannon) – not a very neat image, and not a very neat explanation of it.	*18-20*
Then Malcolm backs away (is Macduff showing signs that he too is ready to explode? How *did* you read *'I am not treacherous'*?)	*20-21*
'Angels are bright…fell': another image of righteousness and damnation.	*22*
Appearances *can* be deceptive; but only because there are men whose appearance is a true reflection of their goodness.	*23-24*
Macduff's response is in the event a despairing rather than a defensive one.	
Malcolm probes again. Why did Macduff leave his family (*'Those precious motives'*) undefended, and hastily *('Without leave-taking')*? Does Malcolm suspect that Macduff has done a deal with Macbeth to	*25-28*

save his own skin? He is quick to cover himself in case Macduff takes offence at that outrageous suggestion (and it is one, rather).   *28-31*

'Knots of love': another way in which people, and a country, can be 'bound together'.

Macduff's reaction is again, however, to despair. This is more of an outburst. Scotland is personified once more as a wounded victim; and Macduff has realised that Malcolm is not the man to stand over (*'bestride'*) and protect her, alongside him. Goodness, the meek goodness of Malcolm, is cowardly; and tyranny is secure (Macbeth would be pleased to hear that). Macduff *is* outraged, too, at Malcolm's suspicion of him, and prepares to leave.   *31-37*

'Check' (line 33): as in check (rein in) a horse (as in the horse of Macbeth's ambition).

Macbeth can *'wear'* his wrong deeds more securely (*line 33*, like the cloak of kingship he has stolen and which has until now sat badly on him).

'Affeered' (line 34) (confirmed in law): legal term. The *'basis'* of Law itself *(line 31)* has been reversed and wrong has become right.

Macduff is playing a cat-and-mouse game with Macduff, soothing him one minute and trying to catch him out the next. He takes up some of Macduff's own ideas.   *37*
o   Scotland is fallen (*'our country sinks'*) – Macduff: *'our down-fallen birthdom' (line 4)*.
o   It is severely injured (*'It weeps, it bleeds'*) – Macduff: *'Bleed, bleed, poor country!' (line 31)*.

His message to Macduff is, 'We're on the same side.' And he is reassuring: he would have support both in Scotland and from England if he opposed the tyrant. But the country would be even worse off with him as King instead of Macbeth, he says.

Here begins the weakest and most tiresome part of the scene. There are those who argue that even though *Macbeth* is the shortest of Shakespeare's plays it could stand to be even shorter…

The poetry is vigorous enough to begin with. Malcolm depicts himself as a plant onto which all sorts of vices have been *'grafted'*. When the flower itself opens he will be revealed as a darker villain even than the *'black Macbeth'*. In *lines 16-17* he represented himself as a lamb; he now makes the mistake of repeating the image. This time it is Macbeth who is the lamb, which leaves Malcolm open to the classic prosecutor's question, 'Were you lying then or are you lying now?'   *51*
52
53-55

He is lying now, of course.

What do you notice about the sound of Macduff's disbelieving response?   *55-57*

It contains
o   alliteration – which as usual carries conviction by adding a 'ring' to the words, and
o   assonance, too (*'hell…evil…devil)* – same effect.

What do you notice about its word order?

The emphatic *'Not'* at the beginning, and the holding back of *'Macbeth'* until the end, the climax, of the sentence

---

Malcolm continues to make things up in support of his case. He agrees ('grants', as if this is some kind of debate) that Macbeth is a bad man; but his list of Macbeth's supposed sins is contrived, and no more than an inaccurate amplification of Macduff's vehement condemnation in the previous lines. *57-60*

Aren't *'false'* and *'deceitful'* the same thing?

'Smacking of every sin /That has a name': exaggeration?

His account of his own lustfulness is no more convincing. He does his best. *60-66*
o   Repeated negatives: *'no...none'*
o   Personalisation : *'your...your...Your...your'*
o   The cistern image: his lustfulness is a deep hole which can not be filled; and in its turn that lustfulness will not be restrained by anything (like a cistern) designed to contain it.
o   He distances himself from himself as if in disgust: *'Such a one'*.

Macduff believes him; but he sees Malcolm's supposedly insatiable lust as only a part of the problem. It is *'boundless intemperance'* in general rather than any specific moral weakness which drives men to evil deeds – an all-embracing desire to have more than your fair share of things, whether those 'things' are women, wealth or power. Note that *'boundless'* and *'intemperance'* are both negatives: they specify an absence of control. It is boundless intemperance which has emptied *'the happy throne'* – the throne of Scotland, Duncan's throne. *66*

68

Malcolm's need for women should be no problem in itself, says Macduff – and here he shows himself to be a pragmatist (a realist, someone who pays more attention to practical considerations than to principles). Malcolm will be able to have all women he wants: there will be plenty of royal groupies willing to give themselves to him just be because he is King. *69-76*

The cynicism of that, and the fact that he is counselling deceitfulness (*'hoodwink...the time'* is hardly any different from *'beguile the time'*, Lady Macbeth's term in *Act One Scene Five line 61*) may not altogether fit the picture of Macduff we would expect Shakespeare to build up at this point as part of his 'planning ahead' – the picture of a man capable, morally as well as physically, of standing up to the tyrant. See, however, the discussion under <u>Character</u>.

What response was Malcolm hoping to provoke in him? Macduff's willingness to accept his (Malcolm's) moral flaws proves nothing: if Macduff is here at Macbeth's behest to persuade Malcolm to return to Scotland so that he can be dealt with, he will be of course try to override Malcolm's objections. Malcolm must try again.

Now that you've had some insight into what's going on here, you can use the next part of the dialogue (*'With this, there grows...'*) as a practice commentary passage. You'll find it set out ready for you at the end of this section (page 111). *76-102*

Malcolm eventually persuades Macduff that he is indeed wholly unfit to rule Scotland. At least there's some life in the dialogue still, at the end of this tortuous passage: *'Fit to govern? /No,not to live!'* Macduff's despair is more believable than Malcolm's efforts to provoke it. Note his *102-3*
o   exclamations
o   repetition of explosive *'t'* sounds (*'not to...untitled tyrant'*)
o   personification of Scotland
o   use of symbol (*'bloody-scepter'd'*)
o   mix of legal and religious terms.

Macduff makes as if to leave, in disgust, for a second time. The fact that he is prepared to do so without trying to persuade Malcolm further is sufficient proof, Malcolm decides, that he has not been *111* sent by Macbeth, and he confesses to Macduff that he has just been testing him. This confession has to be more believable than his pretence, for Macduff's as well as the audience's sake: we all need to know that this is now the 'real' Malcolm, so that the action can move forward. List the methods by which Malcolm (and Shakespeare) try to be convincing.

He
o   praises Macduff *('this noble passion...truth and honour')*.
o   links his suspicions ('**black** scruples') with the *'**Devilish** Macbeth'* – Macbeth has caused them.
o   admits that he has used tricks (*'these trains'* – scent lures dragged on the ground to lead animals into a trap) like Macbeth's.
o   argues that he has just been sensibly cautious (he condemned Macbeth, you will remember, as *'sudden', line 59*).
o   calls upon God to help him and Macduff work together.
o   puts himself in Macduff's hands *('to thy direction')*.
o   uses the informal *'thee'*.
o   seeks in strong terms (*'unspeak...abjure'*) to withdraw the allegations he has just made against himself.
o   lists his virtues: he turns out to be whiter than driven snow, if we are to believe him now (we are supposed to, for Shakespeare's purposes). Note the many negatives.
o   puts himself once more at Macduff's, and Scotland's, disposal.
o   directs Macduff's attention towards Scotland *('whither...')* and suggests they go there as partners *('together')* in a *'warranted quarrel'* (just cause).

Little wonder Macduff shows signs of being confused. Which of the two Malcolms is he to believe?   *137*

'Well, more anon': Malcolm acknowledges that he may have more work to do yet to wholly win   *139*
Macduff over. There's another diversion first (see discussion under *Student Response*) below. It's a
further compliment to King James. Note, in it, only
o   the emphasis on seeing things for yourself (*'which...I have seen him do'*) as the only sure way of   *148-149*
    ascertaining the truth
o   the idea of opposing forces: *'strangely-visited'* – cursed – people are cured by the king's *'**strange**   *150*
    virtue'*; and his power of prophecy matches the Witches'.   *156-157*

Ross's entrance comes as something of a relief to the audience; and Shakespeare makes the most of the   *159*
suspense inherent in the fact that we know he brings terrible news and are soon made aware that he is
reluctant to deliver it.

Malcolm knows Ross is a Scotsman from his clothing, but does not immediately recognise him.   *160*
Macduff sees it is Ross and welcomes him. Malcolm has not realised it is a friend, he says, because   *161*
people are *'strangers'* to (not so much unknown to as mistrusted as a matter of instinct) each other in   *162-163*
these dangerous times.

Macduff's first concern is for Scotland rather than his family – but this is Shakespeare's way of   *164*
postponing the moment when Ross will break the bad news.

We now learn that there has been generalised mayhem in the country, and that Macbeth's cruelties
have gone well beyond the single acts we have witnessed. Scotland is a changed place (*'afraid to know
itself'*): it has lost its character as a *'mother'* and become a mere location for the burial of the dead.   *165-166*
This is a de-personification of Scotland, quite the opposite of what we have seen earlier in the scene.
The only way of being happy there is to know nothing of what is going on.   *166-167*

The *'strange screams of death'* reported by Lenox just after the murder of Duncan *(Act Two Scene Three line 50)*, unreal and unexplained at that time, have now become the cries of real victims, *'shrieks that rend the air'*, so common as to pass unnoticed *('not marked')*. Violence and the extreme feelings *('ecstasy')* of distress that accompany it are now the norm *('modern')*. Scotland has lost her identity, and the identity of those who die and are buried there no longer matters. It is only the good men, it seems, who are dying: they no sooner place a flower in their caps (to indicate their opposition to Macbeth?) than they are killed.

168

171-172

The account is too harrowing in its detail *('Too nice')* for Macduff. Its length makes us wait a little longer for what will be the most fraught part of the scene, when he hears the worst details of all. He moves steadily towards that, asking for *'the newest grief'*, and the audience holds its breath.

174

Ross delays. News is out of date by the time it is given, he says.

175-176

Macduff presses.

177

Ross lies. Then he lies again, about Macduff's children. (How long would an actor pause between each question and its answer?)

In *'they were well at peace when I did leave 'em'* he tries to turn the lies into something approaching the truth, and edges towards breaking the terrible news.

179

Macduff senses his reticence: Ross is holding something back. *'How goes't'* clearly means 'How goes it with my family?' but Ross answers in general terms and tries to turn the discussion. What are *'the tidings'* he has *'heavily borne'* here, however? News about overall events in Scotland? Or the particular news of Macduff's family? If the second of those two, he is hinting to Macduff that more horror is about to emerge, while still failing to speak out.

'Witnessed, the rather': this is not a time for unsubstantiated rumour, Ross knows: he makes it plain that he saw for himself Macbeth's forces moving against those who were *'out'* against him. This *is* a time for action, however: Malcolm needs to be in Scotland raising support. (Note how Ross has turned away from Macduff.)

184

186-188

Clothing image *(line 188)*: even the women of Scotland would fight (with Malcolm) to *'doff'* (throw off) the cloak of sorrow they have been forced to wear.

Malcolm is reassuring (see discussion under <u>Action</u>).

188-191

Ross breaks.

The voices of the play, including the off-stage voices, have been powerful, and terrible. Ross adds one more; this one, he says, is so awful that it should not be heard.

193-195

Macduff guesses, but must still struggle through Ross's prevarications. He does so by seizing on the formal phrase *'pertains to you alone'* and simplifying it into, *'If it be mine, /Keep it not from me.'* Ross is caught, but still hesitates. (Discuss Shakespeare's pacing of this episode: is it too drawn out?)

195-199

199-200

201-203

When the news comes, finally, it comes bluntly.

204-205

But it does not come in detail: Ross forbears *'to relate the manner'* – Macduff found Ross's description of Scotland's general distress *'Too nice' (line 174)*; the precise circumstances of his own family's murder would be too much for him, Ross says. Note, however, the image of slaughtered deer piled on top of each other, with Macduff's carcase on top. Macduff has probably undone with this

205-207

graphic word-picture his own attempts to break the news gently (or at least slowly).

The audience has had to wait for the news to break; we now have to wait for Macduff's reaction to it. This is a powerful moment in the scene, and the stage directions are clear, if implied. Here indeed is a piece of sorrowful apparel that the wearer would willingly *'doff'*. He will however be able to throw it off, Malcolm says, only with words (here) and action *(lines 214-215)*.   *208*

The pathos of this part of the scene rests in the simplicity of Macduff's words and the repetition in his questions.   *211-219*

'He has no children': Malcolm or Macbeth?

> o   If Malcolm, Macduff is speaking to Ross: 'He (Malcolm) can say that because he has no idea what it would feel like to lose his children.'
> o   If Macbeth: 'He has no children, otherwise he could never have inflicted this suffering on me,' or
> o   'He has no children so there is no way I can revenge myself properly on him.'

If you were devising a commentary on this passage, that would be an useful issue to raise in answer to a guiding question like, 'How does Shakespeare convey the depth of Macduff's anguish?' Each interpretation of the line says something different about what Macduff is feeling.

The bird of prey image would be even more useful, however. Note the additional reference to hell and the multiple repetitions and assonance of *'hell...All...all...All?...all...fell'*.

What *is* a man, then? A new answer emerges. Not a creature who can stifle his human (humane) feelings in order to commit bloody acts (Lady Macbeth's view), but a creature who *expresses* his feelings in action.

The feelings themselves however are as important as the action, Macduff insists, and should precede it for a decent length of time. A man must be able to mourn also: *'I cannot but remember such things were.'*   *220*

Guilt has a part too – the guilt of heaven (which did nothing to stop the murders) and of Macduff himself, who caused the problem then ran away (for whatever reason).   *224-227*

Compare Macduff's expression of his culpability here with Malcolm's earlier pretences of guilt. What makes this passage more convincing?

> o   Its brevity
> o   Exclamation (a brief outburst only)
> o   He addresses himself, but doesn't overdo this rhetorical device.
> o   Assonance: *'Naught...Not'*
> o   Alliteration: *'slaughter...souls'*
> o   Prayer

Alright, so his style isn't so unlike Malcolm's. Perhaps it's just the fact that we *know* he has cause which makes the difference.

Malcolm's next image is appropriate to its context.   *228-229*

There's been enough play-acting, in this scene and earlier. Macduff will be himself. This is not a time
for either weeping or bragging. He prays to be able to act *as* himself without delay *('intermission')*. His
outburst is given force by its alliteration.   *232*

The meaning of his final sentence is unclear. It is either   *234-235*
o   'He will only escape if I forgive him; in which case may heaven forgive him also', or
o   'May heaven forgive me (as well as Macbeth) if I let him escape'.

Which do you think is more likely?

'This time': music image ('Your words have a manly beat'; some editions read *'This tune'*: Malcolm's   *235*
whole speech lays emphasis on the natural rhythm of things. The cycle of Creation will run its course.
Macbeth is like a ripe fruit, ready to fall to the ground; and day follows even the longest night.

Overview: other things to note

<u>Setting</u>
o   The world beyond Scotland (England): the contrasts between the two, mainly in the godliness of the one and the
    hell the other has become
o   The world beyond Scotland *('the rich East', line 37)*: a man's honour is worth more than both together, says
    Macduff.

<u>Character</u>
o   Macduff: if he is the pragmatist he seems to be in *lines 69-76*, does that help explain why he ran away from
    Macbeth?

    If he is a pragmatist ('coward' is not a big step further), and is morally suspect (he sees nothing terribly wrong in
    a king deceiving his subjects and using women selfishly), then surely that disqualifies him as the saviour in the
    story, the man who will defeat the villain. We should not be surprised to find, however, that Shakespeare has
    gone beyond stereotype in his characterisations. It is perfectly fitting, and believable, and theatrically 'modern',
    that Macbeth should be defeated finally by a comparatively ordinary man.

<u>Action</u>
o   There's no indication of how long it is since Macduff left Scotland. His first question to Ross *(line 164)*
    suggests it is quite some time; but the impression we have earlier in the scene is that he is newly arrived at the
    English court, which explains Malcolm's suspicion of him. Shakespeare has it both ways.
o   In so far as this play is about conflict (think back to the essay question on page 8) the following consideration
    may be worth noting, since emphasis is placed in this scene on the fact that Malcolm's forces (most of them
    borrowed, but that's not important – they are all on the side of 'Right') will be a match for Macbeth's:
        *'If conflict is at the heart of drama then the opposing forces need to appear counterpoised for some of the
        time at least: points of balance can provide some of a play's more intense moments.'*

    Yes, that could be the starting point for yet another essay question: you can write the instructions yourself.
    A more 'intense' point of balance, of course, is achieved in the moments during which we wait for Ross to
    deliver his news to Macduff...

        'In drama the particular is always more powerful than the general.'

    – another starting-point.

o   Verbal action only, but leading towards military:

'Argument leading to action – the argument giving meaning to the action.'

You could add this scene to the arguments between Macbeth and Lady Macbeth, if you wanted to tackle the question or expand your original response.

Style
o   Clanks, somewhat.
o   The difficulty of telling from the style (alone) of a person's words whether what they are saying is genuine or a pretence. There are ways, however…

Ideas
o   The Bad depends on the Good. Macbeth could not have deceived Duncan if there had been no true men like Banquo *('Though all things foul…must still look so', lines 23-24)* who are what they seem to be.
o   Deceitfulnesss – Malcolm's contrived and 'righteous' pretence, forced on him by the deceitfulness of the time. Fighting fire with fire?
o   Separation and suspicion (Malcolm's failure to recognize Ross)
o   Reputation (Siward's)

Student Response

'That was a long scene.'

'Why doesn't Shakespeare just get on with the story?'

I have to give a longish answer. 'He *is* getting on with it. The Elizabethans saw the matter of kingly virtue as *part* of the story; and part of history also; and part of England's present. Remember that the events described in this play (if they happened at all) predate Shakespeare's own time by some five hundred years. Shakespeare is perhaps, in this scene, trying to say something about issues of importance in the world to which *his* audience will return.'

*****

Additional questions (A Level)

Discuss the idea that Macbeth doesn't really take part in this section of the play, but looms over it nevertheless. Is that a weakness in the action?

'Evil is always more interesting than goodness.' Does Act Four bear this statement out?

Commentary Practice

You're on your own with this next passage (and it's not an easy one)…but an underlined version with notes can be found on page 143, for comparison. Don't worry if your comments are very different from what you find there: the important thing is that you are able to support them by detailed reference to the text.

Sample passage

MALCOLM: With this, there grows

        In my most ill-compos'd affection, such

        A staunchless avarice, that, were I king,

        I should cut off the nobles for their lands,

        Desire his jewels, and this other's house,   *5*

        And my more-having would be as a sauce

        To make me hunger more, that I should forge

        Quarrels unjust against the good and loyal,

        Destroying them for wealth.

MACDUFF: This avarice

        Sticks deeper, grows with more pernicious root   *10*

        Than summer-seeming lust; and it hath been

        The sword of our slain kings: yet do not fear;

        Scotland hath foisons to fill up your will,

        Of your mere own. All these are portable,

        With other graces weigh'd.   *15*

MALCOLM: But I have none. The king-becoming graces,

        As justice, verity, temperance, stableness,

        Bounty, perseverance, mercy , lowliness,

        Devotion, patience, courage, fortitude,

        I have no relish of them; but abound   *20*

        In the division of each several crime,

        Acting it many ways. Nay, had I power, I should

        Pour the sweet milk of concord, into Hell,

        Uproar the universal peace, confound

        All unity on earth.

MACDUFF: O Scotland! Scotland!   *25*

MALCOLM: If such a one be fit to govern, speak:

        I am as I have spoken.

Guiding question (one's enough)

What methods does Malcolm use to test Macduff?

Act Five

Act Five Scene One

Commentary

Time moves on: this is the third might the Doctor and Gentlewoman have watched together; and Macbeth has been *'in the field'* for several nights at least.

3

They both speak in prose: this is real life looking in on Lady Macbeth's spiritual turmoil. Their style of speech is moreover plain and factual, the Gentlewoman's account of Lady Macbeth's actions little more than a list. Lady Macbeth's symbolic sealing of the letter means nothing to the Gentlewoman.

3-6

The Doctor is more analytical, and draws attention to the paradoxes of Lady Macbeth's behaviour (*'slumbery agitation'*) and its unnaturalness (*'perturbation in nature'*). His language is more inquisitorial.

7-10

The Gentlewoman's reluctance to answer his questions is a sign of the times (note her emphatic repetition of negatives – *'Neither...nor...no'*). But it also leaves us in suspense as to what we will hear from Lady Macbeth.

11-13

We are invited to *'stand close'* (stay hidden) alongside the Doctor and Gentlewoman as they watch Lady Macbeth: in this way we are pulled into the action (remember the essay question about corridors down which we can approach plays) – one further way in which minor characters can be used (see also under <u>Character</u> below).

16

The taper (candle) – symbol of?

Lady Macbeth's newly-acquired fear of darkness

'Newly-acquired'? Remember how she *wanted* darkness to descend earlier in the play to hide their treachery.

Darkness – itself a symbol...of the *powers* of darkness, of which in her guiltiness Lady Macbeth is now terrified?

The Doctor and Gentlewoman are used here to illuminate Lady Macbeth's actions (*'You see...What is it she does now? Look...Hark! she speaks...Do you mark that?'*) – not just so that that the audience will be in no doubt as to what is happening (although the scene would be best played in semi-darkness) but to convey the wonderment and horror of these ordinary people at what they are witnessing.

20-26

'Yet here's a spot': we come in on the middle of a conversation she is having with herself, or with Macbeth. It is part of a continual and jumbled replay, from which she has no relief, of the murders they have committed.

The Doctor will make a record of what he hears and sees. The implication is that these events are of political as well as medical importance. (What if anything do you think Lady Macbeth has written down in her letters?)

Note how in this and her following speeches Lady Macbeth jumps back and forward through past events. The chronological as well as the natural order of things has been disrupted. The fragmentation

112

of her syntax (language structure) indicates how 'broken up' her mind is. In the space of a few lines she addresses the spot of blood on her hands, herself, perhaps a general audience *('Hell is murky')*, and Macbeth. With *'who would have thought...in him'* she returns to her present problem, that of washing the blood off her hands. Note her *'Yet'*, a repeat of the *'Yet'* of *line 25*: her mind is running in a loop. *28-32*

'The Thane of Fife had a wife': her sing-song reference emphasises her distracted state of mind, and there's a contrast between its innocent nursery-rhymishness and the horror of the facts. Does she wonder, in *'where is she now?'*, where she herself will be, soon? Then she returns to the problem of the blood on her hands; then she's at the banquet once more. *34*

'Go to, go to': there's some doubt about whether the Doctor is speaking to Lady Macbeth or to the Gentlewoman. What do you think? *37*

Either way this is the judgement of the world, as represented by the Doctor then by the Gentlewoman. Such things should not have been heard (the Doctor, if he is addressing the Gentlewoman); they should not have been spoken (the Gentlewoman); the events the words represent are beyond imagining (the Gentlewoman again). Those plain moral views are expressed in firm and monosyllabic language weighted with echoes. Examine those echoes.

'Go to, go to...known...not...spoke...not...that...knows...known'

The assonance and repetitions continue in Lady Macbeth's lines – *'smell...still...Oh! oh! oh!'* *40-41*

The heart' (not *'her heart'*): the Doctor is struggling to speak in a detached and professional manner; but as a man he is shocked to the core by what he has seen and heard. *42*

'Charged': a discreet weapon image – Lady Macbeth's heart is overloaded with pain, like a cannon with gunpowder, and needs to be *'discharged' (line 61)*.

The Gentlewoman means something slightly different by *'heart'*: to her Lady Macbeth is not a patient but a woman who has paid too high a price for *'the dignity'* (status) of being Queen; and her sympathy this further demonstrated in her feeling response to the Doctor's bemused *'Well, well, well – '*. *43*

'This disease is beyond my practice': it is the practice of the Witches (both their professional practice and their plotting – another sense of 'practice') which has caused it. *47*

The murders of Duncan and Banquo are still confused in Lady Macbeth's mind; and she is still using *'yet'*: in her mind she is going over her argument with Macbeth *'yet again'*. *49-50*

'Even so?': the Doctor is horrified to learn that the King and Queen are perhaps responsible for... *51*

---

the death of Banquo in addition to that of Duncan and Lady Macduff (how much of it all has the Doctor fully understood, in fact?)

The repetitions accumulate in Lady Macbeth's parting lines. *54-56*

The Gentlewoman knows more about the pattern of Lady Macbeth's behaviour; but it is the Doctor who puts that behaviour in context among all the other unnatural things that are happening. His language is loosely but grotesquely medical in its associations – *'Foul...breed...infected...* *57-58*
59 deaf...discharge... annoyance' ('self-harm', looking forward to the suggestion that Lady Macbeth commits suicide).

The Doctor offers an important thought, and an even wider context, in passing. *'God, God forgive us*   *63*
all' suggests that even though Macbeth and Lady Macbeth may have committed these acts of violence,
it is man's general sinfulness which is to blame: even the *'good doctor'* shares in that.   *68*

Overview: other things to note

Setting
o   There are still ordinary people, within a whole country, trying to get on with their lives in spite of the turmoil Macbeth has brought down on them.

Character
o   Gentlewoman: Shakespeare often uses his minor, or 'ordinary', characters to speak with insight about the major events of a play. He does that here, even though the Gentlewoman's cautiousness makes her vague *('She hath spoke what she should not').*
o   Doctor: he speaks with authority as much as with insight, the authority of his profession – which, he admits, Lady Macbeth's ailment is beyond the help of. (Compare the confidence of the English Doctor in *Act Four Scene Three.*) The Doctor and the Gentlewoman, together, add 'perspective' to the present situation. Both, however, also demonstrate a kind of anxious loyalty.
o   Lady Macbeth: does her present broken state, and the loyalty of her two attendants, help modify our perceptions of her? Do we feel anything approaching sympathy?

Action
o   This scene emphasises the fact that Macbeth has lost his only ally, and will have to face his end alone.
o   Note that the scene divisions of *Act Five* are different in different editions. There's a strong argument for running some of them together in a production to give a sense of continuous action as the play moves towards its climax.

Style
o   The use of prose to emphasise the objectivity of the two observers, and, as a matter of convention, Lady Macbeth's madness.

Ideas
o   Paradox: Lady Macbeth seems to be asleep, but she is behaving as if she is awake; she seems to have got what she wanted but is severely unhappy.
o   Inevitability *('What's done cannot be undone')*
o   A simple justice: Lady Macbeth is paying an awful price for her wrong-doing.

General
o   This is the third scene in a row in which we have been shown what is happening at the edges of Macbeth's life, without seeing the man himself.

Student Response

The class note the return to 'spookiness' – the Witches are there in the shadows as Lady Macbeth sleepwalks.

'Shakespeare has used the Doctor and the Gentlewoman very skilfully in this scene. What they don't say is more important what they do. The Doctor's final line *'I think, but dare not speak'* tells us a lot.

'This is what life under under a tyrant is like.' (More than one of the class have lived in a troubled country.)

There's useful material here to include in the essay on minor characters (page 77). There's not a lot of enthusiasm in the class for the project; but I point out that this is a popular question for examiners who want to give credit to the candidates who really know their set texts well, as opposed to the ones who've only looked closely at the main characters.

It's time for an essay anyway, so I give them one for which this particular scene might be a good starting point:

'Poets explore the significance of ordinary things, playwrights investigate extraordinary people or events.'

In what ways are the people or events of the plays you have studied extraordinary? By what means do the playwrights investigate them?

A similar essay on a recent IB paper used the phrase 'individuals of intensity'. Lady Macbeth is certainly one of those, nowhere more than in this scene; and her sleepwalking with all that has caused it is 'an extraordinary event'…but the essay would have to include Macbeth himself, of course, and probably the Witches.

*****

Act Five Scene Two

Commentary

Drums and flags (and *'Exeunt, Marching'* at the end of the scene): the world of the Good has mobilised against Macbeth.

So has the Past. The *'revenges'* (desire for revenge) of Malcolm and Macduff *('the good Macduff')* burn in them as brightly as Macbeth's ambition did once; and their *'causes'* (reasons for action, cases against Macbeth) are so powerful that they would raise the dead (Duncan? Banquo? Lady Macduff? Etc?) against him.   *3*   *4-5*

Everything is coming together *'well'* against Macbeth. The rebellious Scots will meet with the force from England. Shakespeare here provides us with a map of the campaign and a list of those who will participate…and a reminder that Birnam Wood will have a part to play also.   *6*

This is an organised campaign (remember how efficient the Witches have been): Lenox has a *'file /Of all the gentry'*. Shakespeare is emphasising the strength of the forces ranged against Macbeth. They may consist in part of untried (and innocent?) young men; but that is perhaps in their favour – they represent a new Scotland under the leadership of the young Malcolm, determined to do away with this new tyranny before it can become old. So much for Lady Macbeth's 'New Man'.   *8-9*

But Macbeth must not be seen as a *beaten* man yet, if the later stages of the story are to hold up. He is still *'the tyrant'*, a man of power; and Dunsinane is a *'great'* castle *('the opposing forces need to appear counterpoised for some of the time at least')*.

It is not only the opposing forces which can be balanced at some point in a tragedy. In a *sophisticated* tragedy our view of the central figure can be ambivalent. Just how bad, and how mad, a man *is* Macbeth? It depends where you stand, says Caithness: *'Some say…'* (If ever a quotation about a tragic hero was 'made' to be the basis of an essay on him, this is it.)   *13-14*

The image of a distended stomach too big for the belt which fails to encircle it is not very secure. For one thing it runs against the more vivid picture Angus paints in the next speech of Macbeth as a dwarfish figure who cannot fill his stolen clothes. For another its meaning is unclear. Does it refer to   *14-16*
o   Macbeth's *'distempered'* (swollen) ambition, which he can no longer restrain?
o   Macbeth's *'distempered'* (sickly) situation or case *('cause')* which he has lost control of (because his forces are deserting him)?

There are four reasons, Angus says, why Macbeth is now facing destruction. They are?   *16-22*

---

o   He has committed murder.
o   His own rebellion against Duncan has led to rebellion against him.
o   His subjects obey him through fear only.
o   He is not up to the task of being king.

Angus focuses more on Macbeth's state of mind, however, than on his situation in itself. This can only be because Shakespeare wants the audience to focus on it: there is no explanation of how Angus can have gained such insight into what Macbeth is thinking and feeling *'Now…Now…now'*. Why does Shakespeare want the audience to focus on it? (Remember 'dramatists planning ahead'.)

'Sticking': like the blood on Lady Macbeth's hands; like the blood which is too thick to carry feelings

116

of compassion to the heart

'Minutely' (by the minute, incessantly): everything is happening, as we have noted, 'now'.

Menteith penetrates even more deeply into Macbeth's feelings: the tyrant has begun to despise himself for being just that, he says.

The word 'start' has been important throughout the play. We 'start' when we recognise something – a footfall behind us, a face we do not expect to see. Can you remember how the word has been used in earlier scenes? (Do some quick research in a group if that's possible.)
22-24

If you can't recall the examples or find them…here they are. Try to give the speaker and circumstances for each quotation.

> o 'Good Sir, why do you start and seem to fear /Things that do sound so fair?'
> o 'O! these flaws and starts /…would well become a woman's story at a winter's fire'
> o 'Start, eyes!'
> o 'You mar all with this starting.'

> o Banquo to Macbeth when the Witches makes their initial promises (Act One Scene Three lines 51-52)
> o Lady Macbeth to Macbeth after he has reacted violently to the sight of Banquo's ghost (Act Three Scene Four lines 63-65)
> o Macbeth to himself when the Witches show him the line of eight kings (Act Four Scene One line 116)
> o Lady Macbeth to Macbeth as she sleepwalks (Act Five Scene One line 36), recalling his behaviour at the Banquet

What is 'recognised' in each case? And in this latest one (line 23)?

Shakespeare thus continues to prepare us for what we shall find when we encounter Macbeth again. In this, more perhaps than in the question of what will 'happen' now, lies the greatest suspense of the play. What has Macbeth become? And what will he become in the short time left to him?

One thing he is now, according to Menteith, is a man who recognises himself. Recognition is an important idea in tragedy. We'll discuss it later when we look at just what Macbeth may have discovered about himself.

'Well': possibly more than 'So then'; perhaps 'Things will be well' (as in line 6).
25

Caithness's medical imagery carries on from the Doctor's and leads to Macbeth's in the next scene. The idea of purging becomes significant (and is used ironically) there.
27-29

Caithness's enthusiasm (he is happy that they should pour out 'each drop' of their blood to cure the country's ills) is qualified by the more realistic Lenox ('Or so much as it needs…'). When this is all done, there must be a Scotland (a garden – note the imagery) left worth the having. Caithness is no less firm of purpose, however: his alliterative phrase 'Make we the march' indicates that. And 'Birnam' will have an ominous ring about it, now, as far as Macbeth is concerned.

Overview: other things to note

Setting

o   The need for order and the rule of law (the belt image): Scotland is sick.

Character

o   The characters in this scene form a sort of chorus, commenting on Macbeth's situation….

Action

o   …while taking the action forward at a practical level.

Style

o   Less jingoistic (drum-beating) and more thoughtful than we might have had in a less subtle telling of the story. Shakespeare 'analyticises' the situation at this point.

Ideas

o   Righteousness
o   Self-knowledge

General

o   Once again we have been made to wait for Macbeth to appear.

Student Response

'Macbeth doesn't have chance, does he?'

That's the impression we get, the class agree; but we must also feel that he might just escape his fate 'otherwise what's the point in reading the rest of the play?'

That raises a whole lot of other questions (about why we go to the theatre in the first place, why we enjoy having some stories told to us over and over again, and so on). For the moment we concentrate on the one we looked at much earlier in our discussions:

'Dramatists must balance a sense of inevitable consequence in their plays against the possibility of surprise.'

How successfully do the dramatists you have studied do this?

It doesn't take us long to agree that Macbeth's fate has been sealed from the beginning – the Witches have seen to that. So nobody expects him to win the final battle. A better starting quotation might be one designed to be answered by the class when they have read the first half of *Death of a Salesman*:

'By the mid-point in a tragedy, movement towards a disastrous outcome must be well under way; but the possibility of redemption and triumph must still be preserved.'

Discuss the play in relation to the above statement.

We are well past the mid-point of *Macbeth*; but this question does offer another way of ending the story. Macbeth may die, but he could die in such a way that he regains something of what he has lost. A first step towards that might be a realisation of what he has become *(Menteith: 'all that is within him does condemn /Itself...', lines 24-25)*.

'Well if he's going to turn into a good guy he'd better hurry up!'

*****

Act Five Scene Three

Commentary

An actor playing Macbeth could quite justifiably explode onto the stage at the beginning of this scene. (The *'B'* of *'Bring me no more reports'* is what is called a plosive consonant.) Make a list of the methods by which Macbeth shows his confidence (just what a Guiding Question would focus on, so regard this as a mini-exercise if you want).

1-10

> o   The plosive *'B'* as noted
> o   Phrases of extremes *('no more...all')*
> o   Reassurance based on the Witches' prophecies
> o   Dismissiveness of *'the boy'* Malcolm
> o   Emphasis on the Witches' total *('all')* prescience (knowledge of what is to happen)
> o   Weightiness of their statements *('pronounced')*
> o   Direct quotation of what they have said
> o   *'Then'* – draws favourable conclusion from the above
> o   Alliteration *('fly...false')*
> o   Scorn of the self-indulgence of his English enemies
> o   The formal structuring (including the rhyme) of his closing statement

Further exercise: list the methods by which Shakespeare suggests that Macbeth's confidence is ill-founded (there are almost as many – balance once more).

> o   Macbeth's unwillingness to hear the truth *(line 1)*
> o   News that his soldiers *are* flying
> o   Reference to Birnam Wood (see last line of the previous scene: the forces opposing him are to unite there).
> o   His dependence on the Witches: we know they are playing games with him.
> o   Shakespeare's representation of the English, in earlier scenes, as pious and powerful rather than self-indulgent
> o   The contrast between Macbeth's faith in his ability to *'sway'* (control) things *(line 9)* and Caithness's view that he cannot *'buckle'* in either himself or his forces, depending on how we interpret *Scene Two lines 15-16*
> o   *'the heart I bear'*: that (according to Menteith) has been weakened by self-doubt.

So here is another simple irony: the more Macbeth reassures himself, the more vulnerable he seems to be. That parallels a greater irony: the more he has tried to secure his position (by slaughter) the more enemies he has created.

Then he reveals his underlying anxiety by his treatment of the Servant, which is comically cruel.

11-12

Comical? Abuse can be, when it is exaggerated, expressed in powerful and picturesque language, is directed at somebody else, and does no real harm. In these two lines note
o   the sound effects (alliteration; plosive *'d'* and *'b'*, gutteral *'g'*; the assonance of *'goose look'*)
o   imagery of Hell.
o   *'cream-faced'*: another example of the imagery of milkiness and paleness (all equating to cowardice); cream-faced perhaps has the added idea of 'curdled'.
o   the scornful term *'loon'* ('idiot, simpleton'), a word with appropriately Scottish connections

o   the goose image: geese are not just white but easily startled and prone to run around foolishly in circles.

Cruel? The Servant is almost the best of what is left to Macbeth, now that his other servants have fled (remember how he had to make do with riff-raff in the matter of Banquo's murder): he is a helpless, cringing young fellow, and Macbeth does make him run round fearfully.

Analyse for yourself the comic effects of Macbeth's next attack on the Servant.   *14-17*

How does Macbeth himself come out of all that? If we feel that his self awareness has grown (in line with Menteith's claim that he is beginning to despise himself) then we can imagine that this is self-parody: he is playing the bully as a jest at his own expense – his grim humour showing itself once more. The passage could at least be played in such a manner.

Menteith was right. This is now a reflective Macbeth, one who realises what he has lost in the pursuit   *19* of his ambitions. His speech is disjointed as he swings between the needs of the moment (to hear how things stand, and to put on his armour), his sense of how crucial a time is upon him (*'This push /Will cheer me ever, or disseat me now'*), and an expression of his innermost feelings (the bulk of what he says).

'Cheer' (chair)...*disseat'*: this may be a pun. Is he jesting once more? The lines which follow are probably too sombre to support that idea.

He talks like an old man. He *is* old, in experience, or at least in the experience of death.

But just how much responsibility does he accept for what has happened to him? *'My way of life'* does not mean 'the way I have lived', although that is what has brought him to this pass. It's no more than 'the path he has walked', which has led him into the autumn of his days...so there's no clear acknowledgement here that he's brought this unhappiness on himself.

Note the image of natural process (the withering of leaves): he is the victim of time more than anything else, he suggests. The fact that he cannot enjoy the normal comforts of old age is also the fault of those who have deserted him. The best he can hope for is the lip-service (*'mouth-honour'*) of those who remain. There are even the beginnings of self-pity (*'the poor heart'*).

But what about Seyton? Is he there still simply because he's frightened to run away? He seems to have   *30* more about him than that. He calmly stands by the truth of what has been reported, even though it is not what Macbeth wants to hear; and his response to Macbeth's alliterative outburst and his demand that he immediately be armed is practical – *''Tis not needed yet'*. The presence of at least one man who   *33* may have retained some loyalty towards Macbeth is dramatically crucial.

Macbeth's insistence that he put on his armour, and his belligerent vigour, are dramatically *effective*. He gives four quick orders. He is not in the wrong; he will fight to the end.

The Doctor has entered with him in some editions and performances, but enters now in others. What   *37* difference does it make?

If the Doctor has been standing to one side throughout the first part of the scene, and Macbeth turns to him only now to ask about Lady Macbeth, then...what?

'Your patient': a touch of (forced) joviality?

'Thick-coming': coming thick and fast, but with the repeat idea that their thickness is clogging more natural feelings, as well as preventing medicinal sleep.   *38*

'Cure her of that': the fancies or the inability to sleep? *'That'* suggests that Macbeth has firsthand knowledge – and he does, of both fancies and sleeplessness.   *39*

There has been much aggressive questioning in the play. Macbeth now challenges the Doctor professionally. His imagery is mixed – medical, gardening, writing (recalling the letters Lady Macbeth wrote in her sleep) and perhaps weapon (*'stuffed'* associated with *'charged'* earlier). The very length of the question and the richness and variety of its imagery suggests how heartfelt it is. Macbeth needs such medicine as much as his wife. The fact that the Doctor cannot supply it enrages him: *'Throw physic to the dogs.'*   *46*

But the Doctor's reply has been a wise one. Self-cure is the best, the only, remedy.

It is not available to Macbeth, however. He has not gone so far in self-knowledge that he can take responsibility for what he has done and seek ways of putting it right (could there be any?) Capitulation and confession are not options: that would be too unlikely a resolution; so *'Come, put mine armour on; give me my staff'* is his response. The staff is a symbol of whatever authority remains to him. He will exercise it: *'Seyton, send out'* to…

---

hang the faint-hearted.

His preparations are now frantic. The Doctor cannot cure his or Lady Macbeth's mental sickness; can he at least cure Scotland's ills? Macbeth would settle for that.   *50-56*

There is an irony here, however: Macbeth wishes to have the country purged. But it has been poisoned not by the English presence but by his own deeds. Scotland needs to be 'scoured' of *him*.

There is some pathos certainly in the fact that Macbeth asks the Doctor of all people whether he has any news of the English forces: he will take news from anywhere, now.

The Doctor is circumspect: He knows there are English soldiers nearby, he says, because he has seen Macbeth's own army preparing to meet them. That tells Macbeth nothing.

Having decided that aggression is the better part of valour, Macbeth is impatient to fight and leaves, almost comically, with Seyton still trying to fit his armour to him. The Doctor's departure is also light in vein: he is not a stage villain but a stage coward, Robert Bolt's Common Man again. His rhyming couplet echoes and mocks Macbeth's.

Overview: other things to note

<u>Setting</u>
o   The world has grown narrower. Macbeth is hemmed in.

<u>Character</u>
o   Macbeth: there is room for interpretation. He is defiant; but is he blindly and stupidly defiant or heroically so?

<u>Action</u>
o   Macbeth spins himself into a tornado of resistance.

<u>Style</u>

o   Macbeth's language is more direct and resonant in this scene than in any other in the play so far. Pressure brings out the best poetry in him.

<u>Ideas</u>

o   Appearance and reality: Macbeth prefers to believe in his apparent invulnerability rather than face the reality that he is trapped by powerful enemies and his own forces are deserting him. He also tells the Servant to take his frightened face away *(line 19)* as if a face is a transportable (and changeable) thing and he wants him to return with a better one.

<u>General</u>

o   Macbeth's feelings here are mixed; our feelings about him probably are, too.

Student Response

'Macbeth doesn't seem like a dwarfish thief in this scene.'

'Maybe he's started to grow again.'

'Let's see how he dies.'

*****

Act Five Scene Four

Commentary

Macbeth is not the only character to show grim humour: Malcolm's opening comment (a reference to his father's murder) has an ironic touch – part of a process by which Shakespeare develops his character as the man who will soon be king.

Why does Malcolm suggest that they hide their numbers? Does he want it to appear that there are fewer, or more, soldiers marching on Dunsinane? Why?   *4-7*

The real reason, of course, is to…

> allow the Witches' prophecy to come true. But it's unlike Shakespeare not to give us a plausible 'in-play' explanation.

Macbeth is, they believe, still *'confident'*. That's true, isn't it? Note the dramatic effectiveness of this swift switching back and forward between the two opposing sides and their perceptions of each other. Shakespeare gives us a bird's-eye view.   *8*

Macbeth has been abandoned by his followers at all levels *('Both more and less')*: betrayal (which is how he will see it) knows no class. *Is* Seyton a *'constrainèd thing'*? We thought not.   *12*

Macduff, a man with a mission of revenge, has no time for speculation: Shakespeare once more suggests the powerful onward movement of events, as he does also in Siward's speech. The important idea behind both speeches is that the future can only be clearly seen when it becomes the present: outcomes, not possibilities, are what matter. The enormous energy Macbeth and Lady Macbeth put into imagining what the future might hold for them is now shown to have been futile.   *14-16*

In the style of these two speeches, note
o   the terms associated with virtue (in Macduff's lines)
o   the clothing image *('put we on')*
o   alliteration suggesting certainty *('due decision')*
o   emphatic rhyme
o   the strong marching rhythm of Siward's final (short) line.

Overview: other things to note

Setting
o   Birnam Wood: the Witches are about to spring part of their trap.

Character
o   The opposing forces have united; the list of characters is longer.

Action
o   *'Marching'*: the action marches, too.

Style
o   For the main part, plain and business-like

<u>Ideas</u>
o   Appearance and reality (the tree trick)
o   Professional efficiency *('industrious soldiership')*

<u>General</u>
o   The overall impression of men of sound mind behaving soundly, in contrast to the madness inside Dunsinane. Normality is about to swamp unnaturalness.

Student Response

'They're all being a bit cautious, aren't they?'

'That's Shakespeare keeping the suspense going, isn't it?'

We talk about the pacing of events: there is a 'proper' speed at which they should happen, and the concept of dramatic rhythm is almost as important as that of dramatic logic.

*****

Act Five Scene Five

Commentary

'Drum and colours': the balance of opposing forces.

Seyton is still there.

Macbeth *is* confident, as Siward said. How does Shakespeare convey his confidence in *this* speech?   *1-6*

- o   Macbeth orders that banners be hung on the walls in a show of defiance.
- o   He personifies Dunsinane (which, you will remember; is *'great'*): it will laugh at attempts to capture it.
- o   He uses the possessive (and royal) *'our'* three times.
- o   Time is on his side, he says.
- o   So are famine and sickness (which he also personifies, as creatures for which his enemies will become simply food).
- o   He implies that right is still on his side *('those that should be ours')*.
- o   He uses more alliterative *'b'* sounds ('pl......').

You should be pretty good at analysing this sort of passage by now!

The women's cry comes from *'within'* (i.e. from the curtained area at the back of the Elizabethan stage). We should assume that Macbeth is facing forwards, towards the audience. The cry therefore comes from behind him. How does that add to its impact (when we guess, or learn, what it signifies)?

Lady Macbeth dies 'behind his back' – another act of betrayal. Note the simple placing of things on (or off) stage, when it can be symbolic.

Why according to Macbeth is he less fearful to hear such a cry than he would once have been?   *9-15*

Because he has grown accustomed to the sounds of suffering: there is nothing new for him to 'recognise' (*'start'* at) in such an event.

'Dismal treatise' is interesting. It suggests that life for Macbeth is becoming a story to which he is listening. That in its turn implies a loss of control over events: he can merely await their outcome. We are to learn in what are perhaps his most memorable lines that when the story comes to an end it will have meant nothing.

Note:
- o   The food images *('taste...supped')*
- o   The sense of time passing, and things changing *('The time has been')*
- o   The reference to cooling (in contrast to the heat of his earlier ambition)
- o   *'night-shriek'*: Another of the play's off-stage voices
- o   The idea of dead things (his hair) rising
- o   The wash of sound in *'direness, familiar to my slaughterous thoughts'*, almost as if his mouth is

half-full of the blood he has *'supped'* (yes, that *is* a bit too fanciful).

'She should have died hereafter': two meanings are possible:
17-28
o   She would have died at some time in the future anyway (so it doesn't much matter that she's died now).
o   There would have been a better time for her to die (i.e. after all of this is over).

Which one leads more neatly into the next line, *'There would have been a time for such a word'* ('This news could have come at a more appropriate moment')?

> The second one

Which one is a better match for the remainder of the speech?

> The first one

Which one shows Macbeth to be more uncaring about her death?

> The first one: the second one does at least imply that he would have wanted her around a little longer to give him whatever support she could.

We don't have time in the theatre to stop and ponder such things, of course. It's very much up to the actor to decide how much if any sorrow he shows. The remainder of Macbeth's speech is certainly a lament, but for all of mankind, not just for his wife. It expresses a desperate sense of loss, but not loss of a person, more loss of a meaning.

But the power of the poetry! It's as moving as Othello's words over the body of Desdemona. You'll be a lucky candidate if you're given such a rich passage to comment on.

Even the uncertainties of meaning in the opening two lines *('She should...such a word')* prepare us for the theme at the heart of the speech – that of life's senselessness.

Try answering the following questions, which will take you a long way towards producing a commentary of your own on this key passage.

(You'll note how we're getting you to do more of and more of the work now. It's not that we're running out of ideas; the fact is that *your* ideas, the ones you develop for yourself, will be more useful to you than any we can offer. Now that you've learnt what to look out for, preparing a passage for commentary should be easy. Fun?)

o   *'Tomorrow...'*: comment on the sound of this word and its repetitions
o   What about the fact that there are only three stressed syllables in that line?
o   Why *'creeps'*?
o   Why *'creeps **in**'* (as opposed to 'on', which is nearer to the sense meant)?
o   *'this'*: does Macbeth gesture as he speaks this word? Walk across the stage? Walk how?
o   *'petty'* just means 'small' (as in small steps). How does our more modern understanding of the

word fit in with the sentiments of the passage?
o *'day to day'*: how is this phrase linked to the repeated 'tomorrows' in both sound and meaning?
o *'the last syllable of recorded time'*: connections with other similar images and references?
o *'all our yesterdays'*: the effect of this phrase in conjunction with his 'tomorrows'? Think about time stretching forward and backwards. Think about *'All'*. Remember *'All our nights and days to come', Act One Scene Five line 67.*
o *'lighted'*: days = ? The picture that phrase puts in our mind?
o *'our'*: whose?
o *'fools'*: who?
o *'dusty death'*: why dusty? Any special effect in the alliteration?
o *'Out, out'*: gesture?
o *'candle'*: = ?
o *'shadow'*: predominant idea – a shadow is............ Secondary idea – a shadow is.............. (Any other ideas?)
o Why a *'walking'* shadow?
o *'poor player'*: a .... actor (consider alternative meanings for *'poor'*)
o *'struts and frets'*: carries on the idea of .... Has Macbeth strutted at any point? Has he fretted? What's the effect of the phrase's assonance (repeated sounds)?
o *'his hour'*: suggests that life is ?
o *'the stage'*: = ?
o *'And then is heard no more'*: effect of these quiet monosyllables?
o *'tale /Told...idiot'*: effect of the long vowel and the repeated *'t'*?
o Antithesis in the last two lines?
o *'Nothing'*: picks up on ? two lines before.

All we've done above is note (pretty well all) the words and ask you what they mean or suggest and why the writer (WS) has used them. That's just what you need to do for yourself when you read *anything* that may affect you, whether it's an advertisement or a political speech or an exam question.

A sudden change now takes us beyond this powerful protest from Macbeth (on all our behalfs) about the purposelessness of our existence. Sometimes life is ultimately, in Siward's words from the previous scene, no more than an *'issue strokes must arbitrate'*. There is nothing left but to fight. You can thereby achieve, if not understanding, at least an end. The change lies in Macbeth's next words, almost as scornful as those he lashed the Servant with in *Scene Three*. The abbreviated (verbless) phrase *'thy* **29** *story quickly'* adds to the alteration in mood. There is a quickening from here onwards. And there is a stumbling – Macbeth's fierceness causes the Messenger to fall over his words and Macbeth must again prompt him: *'Well, say, sir.'* There is room once more for dark comedy. The Messenger begins rather **32** long-windedly. Perhaps he also is a poor soul, a *'constrainèd thing'*, too cowardly even to run away. Macbeth's glowering forces him quickly to his conclusion; Macbeth's outburst (*'liar and slave!'*) makes him repeat himself, plaintively. **35**

All that matters now, for the audience, is how Macbeth will behave. That is more important than what will happen to him.

Is there humour in his reference to *'the next tree'* on which he will hang the Messenger if he is lying? **39** (His meaning in that case: 'If there are no trees coming towards us we will go out and find one to hang you from.') There is confidence, certainly, not only that he will be able to leave Dunsinane to find such a tree, but that he will be in power long enough for the Messenger to starve to death suspended from it.

Confidence, that is, if the Messenger is lying. Then comes the other *'if'* in this balanced sentence. The **40** assonance of *'speech...sooth...much'* gives point to the alternative, which is despair and resignation because the Messenger is right. Macbeth has been riding on the back of his belief in the Witches' prophecy; he would, if Birnam Wood were indeed moving, have to *'pull in'* (rein in) his determination to fight and give way to fear of the devil's deceitfulness (*'equivocation'*, taking us back to all the Porter had to say on the subject). He will have been tricked, he realises. He speaks with almost a naïve wonderment in his repetitive: *'Birnam Wood...come to Dunsinane...and now a wood /Comes towards Dunsinane.'*

42
43
44-46

Then he makes a bad choice. He could have stayed in the heavily fortified castle. Instead he goes out to meet his enemies.

'How far does Macbeth contribute to his own downfall?'

That would be a rather stodgy A Level question; and you'd need to avoid getting entangled in a philosophical discussion of whether Macbeth could in any case have avoided what is fated for him.

The logic of his decision is not clear. But dramatically Shakespeare needs to get him out into the open.

47-48

Shakespeare does make something of an effort to explain why Macbeth abandons his stronghold. It is not after all a matter of logic or strategy. It is a matter of despair: *'I 'gin to be aweary of the sun.'* (Note the abbreviations of *''gin'* and the others which follow: he is too weary even to fully form his words.) It is not however a matter of surrender. He would choose instead to bring *'th' estate o' th' world'* down around his ears – the supreme act of destruction of a destructive man. He said, much earlier in the play *(Act Three Scene Two lines 16-19)* that he would rather *'let the frame of things disjoint'* than live in fear; now he says he would rather let them disjoint than live at all. This is almost suicidal talk; and his decision to leave Dunsinane is in effect a suicidal act. It is accompanied by words of explosive defiance, made even more powerful by their rhyming.

49

Overview: other things to note

<u>Setting</u>
o *'Within the castle'*: but Macbeth can hear the shouts *('They come!')* on the battlements. This is the knocking on the gate again: justice approaches.
o *'A cry...of women'*: there is still a community here, of sorts.

<u>Character</u>
o Macbeth: the violent swings of his emotion, each one caused by voices he hears or news which is brought to him. Is his response (at a personal level) to Lady Macbeth's death as off-hand as it seems?
o Seyton: continued loyalty, if it *is* that

<u>Action</u>
o A last deep breath before the quick-fire final scenes

<u>Style</u>
o Can we identify a 'Macbethian style' i.e. one we can see as especially his? Make a list of its characteristics.

<u>Ideas</u>
o The paradox of life: it is both long and short.

<u>General</u>
o Our feelings towards Macbeth?

Student Response

'Macbeth philosophises a lot in this scene. Is that what you meant when you said a play could have a philosophical setting as well as a geographical one and so on?'

'An opinion about life expressed by one of the characters at a particular point in the play doesn't really qualify as a setting. What would, do you think?'

'An opinion about life which most of the people in the play have.'

'Is there one?'

'Most of the people in the play thought life was pretty good when Duncan was king. They're fairly certain it will be alright again once Macbeth has gone.'

'I think it's more the dramatist's opinion about life.'

'What's Shakespeare's opinion about life?'

'That it's sad.'

'It's dangerous.'

'It's both short and long.'

'There are things in it that we can't understand.'

'It goes on.'

'So there's no one message about life that Shakespeare is trying to put across?'

'Not really. It's just life.'

> *'Theatres are not classrooms and plays are not lessons. A good play does not try to teach us any one thing.'*

> *Show how the plays you have studied raise possibilities but avoid judgements.*

We try to list the 'possibilities' suggested by the play (not easy because the word's a bit vague).

Then we discuss 'judgements'. We've just talked about justice approaching Dunsinane, so we seem to be accepting that Macbeth is being judged.

'Ah, but who is judging him? Malcolm and the others, yes. But Shakespeare? The audience?'

The matter of sympathy for Macbeth is related, and needs to be considered.

*****

Act Five Scene Six

Commentary

'Now, near enough': crisp, functional phrasing.

These are the 'good' men *('worthy...noble...worthy')*.

They are also efficient *('our first battle...what else remains to do...our order')*.

Malcolm is already using the royal *'we'*. That's Shakespeare's doing, as part of the process of...

1-6

> building up Malcolm's character and moving towards the re-establishment of rightful kingship...
> and rounding off the play.

Siward's reply is rather meaningless. Think of it as more beating of the drum.

6-8

Same with Macduff's lines. But there is more power in them: note the contrast between the ponderous Latinate phrase *'clamorous harbinger'* and the blunt Anglo-Saxon *'blood and death'*. Formalities (trumpets) prepare the way for finalities.

9-10

Overview: other things to note

Setting
o   *'The plain before the castle'*: things are coming out into the open.

Character
o   Macduff: he is given the job of rounding off the scene in preparation for his re-entry later in pursuit of Macbeth.

Action
o   The scene's shortness

Style
o   Briskness of the language

Ideas
o   Reality (the soldier's numbers) is eventually made plain.

Student Response

'Uh-huh', 'Oh-oh' (pronounced in a variety of ways).

*****

Act Five Scene Seven

Commentary

Macbeth personalises the conflict. By *'They'* we presume he means Malcolm, Siward and so on. Could he possibly, however, mean the Witches?

The predominant idea in the bear-baiting image is that of helplessness *('I cannot fly.')* What other ideas can you find?

> o   Loss of dignity
> o   Unfairness
> o   Madness. The bear would be taunted until it was enraged.
> o   The suggestion (in *'course'*, which is technically only one round of the fight) that this is not the end for Macbeth. But 'course' has a wider meaning (as in 'the sun has run his course'…and Macbeth has already said he is tired of the sun.

Even at the stake he will be safe, Macbeth reassures himself. But if he believes it is the Witches who have brought him here…   *2-4*

'Thou'lt be afraid to hear it': some pride, still? Pride only in the fear his name will arouse.   *5*

As far as the action is concerned, Young Siward is just a dog that has come across the bear prematurely, part of the dramatic warm-up for the real fight. He is used to enlarge Macbeth (in his references to Satan): this is no ordinary creature he faces.

Again it is the fear he inspires which Macbeth is most proud of. He does not acknowledge that Young Siward *has* proved him a liar (by fighting him): *'Thou wast born of woman'* is probably dismissive,   *9* given the two lines which follow. *'Brandished'* suggests that…

> any weapons drawn against him will be waved uselessly.

Noises off stage are significant once more. They have indicated horrors before, they signal horrors (the   *14* presence of Macbeth) now.

Does Macduff hope Macbeth will hear him when he calls out? Not above the noise of the battle, surely. So this is for dramatic effect? Yes, but part of that effect may lie in the suggestion that the more-than-human Macbeth will hear the shout, from wherever he is.

It is Macduff's responsibility to avenge his family. It is also his responsibility to act honourably (and not kill *'wretched Kearnes'*): he must be a fitting instrument of justice. His sword is now dedicated to   *17* the task of killing Macbeth. Note the onomatopaeic battle sounds *('unbattered…clatter… note… bruited')*.

He prays to Fortune; but Fate has already taken care of the matter.   *22-23*

Out of confusion comes victory: Macbeth's soldiers have fought both for and against him; meeting the invaders they have either turned to fight alongside them *('beside us')* or aimed their weapons to miss . Does it matter which interpretation we choose?

Possibly. Any of Macbeth's soldiers turning to fight against him would be at major risk if he eventually won; soldiers only pretending to fight for him would be hedging their bets – a wise course of action in this still uncertain situation.

The *'noble thanes'*, in contrast to what is either disloyalty or duplicity in Macbeth's forces, *'do bravely'* – perform courageously and honourably. *'The day'* is personified as having given itself to Malcolm (as the country has). *'Do'* (in *'do bravely'*), however, has reminded us that all is not yet over, and *'almost'* reinforces that.

26

What's the effect of the *'This'* at the beginning of the first line of Siward's speech together with the *'The'* which begins each of the next three lines?

They add an air of measured certainty to what he says.

It is proper that Old Siward, *'An older and better soldier none /That Christendom gives out' (Act Four Scene Three lines 191-192)* should invite Malcolm, ceremonially (look at his word order), to enter the castle. This is part of the legitimisation (dramatically) of Duncan's successor.

29

Overview: other things to note

<u>Setting</u>
o   *'Another part of the plain'*: Macbeth has gone out to meet his fate.

<u>Character</u>
o   Macbeth: back to his bad old ways
o   Malcolm: embracing his good new ones

<u>Action</u>
o   Suspense: Siward's son has been killed, and when we see Siward himself at the end of the same scene he is yet to be told. So there's irony in his news that, *'the castle's gently rendered'*, as if there has been little loss of life.

<u>Style</u>
o   No long speeches

<u>Ideas</u>
o   There is a price to pay (Young Siward's death) for restoration.

<u>General</u>
o   The skilful way in which the audience is carried from one part of the action to another; and the contrasts between the different parts.

Student Response

'Is anybody having fun in this scene?'

'The audience should be, that's why they're there.'

We talk about the 'fun' of going to the theatre, even when we see some horrible things happening on stage.

*****

Commentary

What or who has suggested to Macbeth that he should kill himself as a matter of honour? The idea is a sort of cultural equivalent to an anachronism (something out of out of place time-wise). It doesn't fit and Macbeth rejects it. His determination to fight on is much more rugged, more 'Highland' if you like. The way in which he expresses it is however typically (for him) brutal. *'Whiles I see lives'* suggests that his killing will be indiscriminate; *'Do better on them'* makes the gashes seem a fashionable adornment.   *2-3*

'Turn, hell-hound, turn!': powerful symmetry.

Why has Macbeth avoided Macduff? For the same reason he now gives for not wanting to fight him? What might that add to our perception of Macbeth's character?

> The idea that he is after all capable of remorse. Would that come as a total surprise?

'Charged': as previously, loaded with, weighted down by; but with an added legal meaning.   *5*

'My voice is in my sword': words, like *'thoughts speculative'*, must sooner or later give way to *'strokes' (Scene Four lines 19-20)*. Life is at its end only a physical thing. Macbeth himself has already decided that. So he fights.   *7*

But he fights his way to a moment's respite during which he tries to persuade Macduff against continuing. This is more than just a boast, then? Has he really had enough of pointless killing? Does he truly feel guilty about the death of Macduff's family?   *8-13*

In the sword-play, will he have fought only defensively, or will he have tried to kill Macduff? Note his self-delusion: he has become as insubstantial as the *'intrenchant air'*, one almost, he thinks, with the spirits who have promised him invulnerability; his life is *'charmèd'* (but does *'must'* rather than 'can' suggest some doubt?)

Macduff's response is more a challenge to Evil than to Macbeth: 'Let the 'angel' (demon) you serve speak the truth, for once.'

'Untimely': Macbeth complained earlier that time moves on too slowly *'from day to day'*; but it can sometimes move too quickly, as in the *'untimely'* birth of Macduff, and what is about to become Macbeth's untimely death.   *16*

Macbeth can only curse…but note that he does not curse the whole man Macduff (whom he has tried to avoid fighting) but only his tongue, which has carried such bad news. The man himself he will refuse, once more, to fight. His quarrel is with the *'fiends'* (the Witches? The powers which control them?) And it is that they 'juggle' – both play with words (*'in a double sense'*) and defy the laws of nature (which is what jugglers do, and what Birnam Wood and Macduff – and Banquo – have done).

The effect of *'these'* in *'these juggling fiends'*?

Macbeth sees himself as surrounded (and mocked?) by the spirits who have tricked him.

The audience too may have expected the Witches to be 'in at the kill'. Might Shakespeare have considered bringing them back on stage at some point, do you think? Does *'these'* indicate that Macbeth may be having another vision?

There's been in interesting shift in Macbeth's understanding of what the Witches promised him. What they said was, *'none of woman born /Shall harm Macbeth' (Act Four Scene One lines 80-81)*. By *Act Five Scene Three lines 6-7* Macbeth is reassuring himself that *'no man of woman born /Shall e'er* **have power**' over him, which is a slightly different thing. In the present scene we find that although his life itself may have to *'yield'* (as in *line 12*) to a man, he himself will not *'yield'* (as in *lines 23 and 27*) his *freedom* to one. The witches' prophecy may have failed him in one sense; but he has taken it over and extended it into one that he can make work – by dying, as nearly as he can, honourably. If we're looking for a way in which Macbeth redeems himself, then this is probably it.

Macduff shows a grim humour of his own, in his description of a Macbeth captured and displayed. How does he set about provoking Macbeth to fight?

By
o   commanding him as if he already has power over him *('Then yield thee')*
o   calling him a coward
o   promising him that he (or his picture) will be put on show
o   indicating that it will become fashionable to laugh at him *('gaze o' the time')*
o   repeating the scornfully plosive *'p'* in *'Painted upon a pole'*
o   indicating that the only public acknowledgement he can now expect is to be raised up high and labelled *'tyrant'*

Macbeth replies with a scornfulness of his own. *'Young Malcolm'* is still the *'boy Malcolm'* of *Scene Three*. The people who would come to look at a Macbeth on show would be no more than *'rabble'* come to watch a bear being *'baited'*. This particular bear will keep more dignity than that, Macbeth vows. Even though he has lost the protection of the Witches' prophecies he will *'try the last'* (put his fortune to the final test – by fighting Macduff).

28

29

32

It's interesting that he makes a point of raising his shield but says nothing about his sword. Does he aim blows at Macduff now, even if he did not do so earlier? If not, is it because he is still hindered by his guilt? (Notice also that he invites Macduff to strike *him*. *'Lay on, Macduff'* means 'Do your worst…and I will endure it.') Possibilities here for a new view of his character, or at least of his death.

Overview: other things to note

Setting
o   This must be a place apart from the rest of battle (a quieter place?): the forces in conflict are greater than military, and this climax deserves total focus. Most directors will dispense with the exeunt and re-entry, and the *'Alarms'*. There is no need for alarms here.

Character
o   Macbeth: as noted

<u>Action</u>
o   The climax (also as noted). What's a climax?

<u>Style</u>
o   The words do, after all, speak louder than the swords.

<u>Ideas</u>
o   The gap that can exist between the spirit *('hope')* and the letter *('word of promise')* of something that is said (Appearance and Reality again, in other words)

<u>General</u>
o   Is Macbeth's death 'big' enough to match his life?

Student Response

'Macbeth couldn't have killed himself anyway, if he was "born of woman".'

*****

'We only see a bit of Macbeth from now on, so perhaps this is this a good a time to talk about what kind of man he died. We've talked about him growing and shrinking; does he ever grown big enough to be called a tragic hero?'

'What does a character in a play need in order to be called a tragic hero?'

'Failure, and probably death; but other things as well. Importance. Stature. A tragic flaw.'

'What's a tragic flaw?'

'"A single human weakness which causes the downfall of a great man – usually through an error of judgement," is the short answer. Sometimes the circumstances of the situation play on the character's flaw to bring about the tragedy.

'Macbeth is the tragic hero of this play because he is the central character and a man of stature, and he is brought down as result of his own weakness (ambition – although some would argue, instead, an inability to take his own decisions and stand by them). He suffers a fall which also brings disaster to others.'

'What do you mean by a fall?'

'A fall from power. A fall from grace. A fall into madness. A fall in the regard of the world.'

'Is Lady Macbeth a tragic hero (heroine) as well, then?'

The class check her against the list. She comes out not as a tragic heroine but as one of the circumstances which play on Macbeth's tragic flaw.

In the end, we say, it becomes a matter of semantics – 'It all depends on what you mean'. The important thing is not how we define 'tragic hero' and whom we might include in the definition. As an audience we should be more concerned with how Macbeth and Lady Macbeth reach us as people. It's worth taking another look an earlier essay question:

> *'Poets explore the significance of ordinary things, playwrights investigate extraordinary people or events.'*

In what ways are the people or events of the plays you have studied extraordinary? By what means do the playwrights investigate them?

We need not worry too much about whether Macbeth is a tragic hero or Lady Macbeth a tragic heroine, or about the ways in which they may be tragic. Labels are useful, but only when they help us to see things more rather than less clearly – things, and people, and the connections between them. The *extraordinariness* of people (real and imagined) is more important than how we choose to categorise them. That's why what we have called stature is crucial.

We do feel sorry for Lady Macbeth and Macbeth, some of the class agree, if that's what is meant by being 'reached' by them. Others find that hard.

I suggest that Shakespeare shows compassion for all of his characters, and ask whether 'compassion', might be a better word than 'sorry' to describe what some members of the class feel. There's a difference: compassion is a larger feeling than 'sorriness', or even pity. I give them a quotation to think about, the novelist Arnold Bennet's note:

'Essential characteristic of the really great novelist: a Christ-like, all-embracing compassion.'

If of a really great novelist, why not of a really great dramatist? Why not of a really great audience?

Compassion may be too strong a term for what we as the audience feel for Macbeth and his wife (and I sense it is, for most of the class); and perhaps 'pity' is too. 'Sorry' is about right.

Isn't 'terror' therefore too powerful also? We talked much earlier about the feelings of 'pity and terror' Aristotle said we should experience when we watch a tragedy. Some of us will feel no more than disturbed by what we have seen and heard. That's ok, I tell the class: one of the prime things about great literature is that you must take it as you find it, and take from it what you can. If the events of the play disturb you but don't terrify you, if you feel sorry rather than compassionate…or if you feel nothing at all…then that's not a failure, either in you or in the play. That's just what happens when you bring together these two things (you and the play, or rather you at this time in your life and this reading or that production of the play.

*****

Act Five Scene Nine

Commentary

Malcolm now needs to be 'sold' to us as a fitting heir to the throne. So Shakespeare lets him begin by showing concern for his *'friends'* – using the royal *'we'*. He is his father's son in more ways than one.

Not a lot of fuss is made of those who have died in the battle. Siward's words are almost off-hand *('Some must go off')*; and we might regard this as dramatic irony, since he is about to learn of the death of his own son and that could be expected to change his tune; but he does not show much more feeling when he hears that Young Siward has been killed. This is all stern, soldierly stuff. All that seems to matter is that Siward's son died bravely. *2*

Why is the fact that it was Macbeth who killed him not mentioned?

> Shakespeare seems to be trying to keep this final scene uncluttered. The identity of Young Siward's killer could be made relevant and dramatically interesting, but only by considerable discourse.

How to round off the play, then? With platitudes about death and honour (we've had those). Then with shocking visual proof that the shocking man Macbeth is indeed dead. Then with an announcement *('Hail, King! For so thou art')* and some ceremonial language paying compliments to all *('compassed with thy kingdom's pearl')*. Then with a round of acclamation. All of that from Macduff. *20-25*

Malcolm, properly, has the last word. The sight of Macbeth's head was, to Siward, *'newer comfort'* – it marked the arrival of a newer Scotland under Malcolm's rule. All Malcolm has to do here is make promises; *do* something new (create Scotland's first earls) as a token of his intentions; plan to apply justice; label and dismiss Macbeth and Lady Macbeth; acknowledge God's hand in events; thank everyone; and invite them all to his coronation.

He does it with some smoothness. The only bits we may notice particularly are the ones that mention Macbeth and Lady Macbeth. After all, they are the only interesting characters in the play, aren't they?

Overview: other things to note

Why not show the world some of the skills you've learnt? Try adding your own overview of the scene, using the five headings. It won't be easy – but we'd love to have your ideas (wordsmith@clix.pt), and may be able to include them in in the next edition of the resource.

Student Response

The class don't want to talk about this tame scene. They want to discuss the Macbeths some more. Did *'the dead butcher and his fiend-like queen'* learn anything?

Not in time, we decide. Hindsight *is* a wonderful thing, but you need a chance to develop it, and Macbeth and his wife are overtaken by events despite all their murderous galloping.

'Surely they learnt not to trust the Witches?'

'Only after they'd trusted them too much.'

'But don't they discover things about themselves?'

Macbeth maybe, Lady Macbeth maybe not, the class decide.

'Do mad people even *know* themselves?'

So this prime essay question probably doesn't apply too well to *Macbeth,* beyond Macbeth's two fine speeches in *Act Five* about the meaningless of life, and of his life in particular:

> *'Self-discovery has replaced discovery as one of Drama's most powerful features.'*
>
> *Discuss the ways in which dramatists present the processes of both discovery and self-discovery..*

Time for another little lecture (I generally try to avoid those). The characters in the world's great plays find out more about themselves than they do about things outside them. In tragedies they find it out too late. They see at the point of discovery what was there to be seen from the beginning, but by then nothing can be done. Macbeth (and Lady Macbeth too – why excuse her?) should have known earlier (and better) than they did what they paid a very heavy price to find out. We should all know better than we do: this is Shakespeare's judgement; but it takes nothing away from his total compassion for us in our benighted state.

I offer the advice that if in the exam the class get a questionable statement like the one about self-discovery, or at least one that doesn't apply to the plays they have studied, they shouldn't be afraid to say either that it's questionable or that it doesn't fit (as long as they can do so at appropriate length).

I also counsel against getting tangled in long discussions about the theory of tragedy, or drama: they need to write about the plays.

*****

Practice Commentary 5

If you answered most of the questions about that wonderful passage in *Act Five Scene Four (lines 17-28)* you gathered more than enough material for a general commentary on it. All you need to do now, if you feel you still need more commentary practice, is to write it out (if that's what you'll have to do in an exam) or deliver it into a tape recorder or a friend's ear. Give some thought first as to how you'll introduce it (put it in context) and round it off (say what's most significant or powerful about it).

Here's a further exercise which will help you give some focus to your commentary. If you're an IB candidate it will offer you invaluable insight into how examiners look at a passage when they're devising their fiendish Guiding Questions.

Look back at the notes you made on the passage. Do you see any links among the questions you were asked or the things you said? Are there any other features of the passage you think are important?

You'll probably come up with a list something like the following.

o   The central line of argument running through the speech
o   The sounds of the passage
o   The images
o   The diction (choice of words, beyond just the images or sound-effects)
o   Macbeth's state of mind
o   Links with other parts of the play
o   An actor's scope for interpretation and gesture

138

Now write a guiding question for each of your topics (or ours). Here are some in case you get stuck..

o   How does Shakespeare give cohesion to the line of thought running through this speech of Macbeth's?
o   How do the sounds of the poetry in this passage contribute to its effect?
o   Show how the images of the passage add to both its meaning and its dramatic impact.
o   What do you find interesting about the diction of the passage?
o   By what methods does Shakespeare convey Macbeth's state of mind at this point in the play?
o   Discuss the links between this passage and the overall themes and events of the play.
o   How much room for interpretation, by either an actor or an audience, is there in this scene?

See? There's nothing much to it. These aren't all, strictly, good IB commentary questions. But they're good questions.

Additional questions (A Level)

How far does Macbeth redeem himself in the manner of his dying?

In what ways is the conclusion of 'Macbeth' satisfying?

Further Essay Questions (IB)

(Most of these can easily be converted into worthwhile A Level or AP questions.)

1. What do you think makes for a successful opening to a play? Illustrate your answer by referring to plays you have studied.

2. How important is it to be able to detect a difference between life as it is lived at the beginning of a play and life as it will be lived after the play has ended? By what methods do dramatists seek to emphasise such a difference?

3. 'A play is in the end a mechanical thing which must work on the stage.'

   What characteristics of the plays you have studied would make them 'work' well in performance?

4. Show how dramatists, in plays you have studied, either maintain a similar style of dialogue throughout or seek to introduce variety in the way their characters speak. What is the effect of either (or both) techniques?

5. 'When you read a play you remain up to a point in control; when you watch a play on the stage you give up much of that control.'

   Discuss that and other differences between reading and watching a play.

6. 'A play must challenge its audience, otherwise it is nothing more than entertainment.'

   In what ways do the plays you have studied challenge their audiences?

7. Most plays have in them some kind of duality – cruelty/kindness, stupidity/wisdom, freedom/enslavement and so on. Discuss the 'dualities' of the plays you have studied.

8. Plays often tell the story of our continuing struggle to either gain or resist power. Show how this struggle is expressed in your selected plays.

9. Every good play has a distinctive dramatic style. What is the dramatic style of each of the plays you have studied?

10. Imagine you are producing each of the plays you have studied. Would you include an interval in all of your productions? Where in each play would you insert it? Justify your choices.

11. What do the endings of the plays you have studied have in common? In what ways are they different?

Further A Level Questions

(These are general essay questions of the Type 5 variety)

1. Scotland herself figures as a character in *Macbeth*. Discuss Shakespeare's interest in the nature of good kingship and how important it can be to the well-being of the ruled kingdom.

2. 'Without its supernatural dimension this play would be tame.' Do you agree?

3. *Macbeth* is a cautionary tale. Show how that influences the way Shakespeare tells the story.

4. Discuss the suggestion that Duncan's murder happens too early in the play, and that Macbeth's downward slide begins before he is fully established as a man of worth.

5. What is Macbeth's tragic flaw?

6. 'The closer a man approaches tragedy the more intense is his concentration of emotion upon the fixed point of his commitment, which is to say the closer he approaches what in life we call fanaticism' (Arthur Miller). How accurate an account does this quotation provide of the changes we see in Macbeth as his story develops?

7. 'We can easily forgive a child who is afraid of the dark; the real tragedy of life is when men are afraid of the light.' What insights does this quotation (NOT by Plato) offer into Macbeth's story?

8. How far is Lady Macbeth responsible for Macbeth's downfall?

9. Discuss the contribution made by the soliloquies and asides of *Macbeth* to the audience's understanding of the play.

10. Which of the play's major themes are expressed mainly through its imagery?

11. 'The poetry of struggle is the most powerful poetry in the play.' Discuss this view.

12. 'The play is about how nothing in this world can be relied on.' Do you agree?

13. *Macbeth* is not so much a revelation of evil as an affirmation of virtue. The evil, however, is dramatically more interesting than the virtue.' Discuss both parts of this statement.

Advanced Placement Free-Response Questions

You will be expected to write three 40-minute essays – usually an analysis of a poem or a pair of poems, a detailed commentary on a prose passage, and a more general essay about a novel or play you have studied. Here are some examples of the type of essay you will be asked to write about the novel or play. In each case you can use *Macbeth* as the work on which you base your answer.

1. F. Scott Fitzgerald wrote, 'Show me a hero and I will write you a tragedy.'

   Select a novel or play in which a major character exhibits heroic qualities but suffers a tragic downfall. Examine the relationship between the character's heroic qualities and his or her downfall. Pay particular attention to any irony the novelist or dramatist reveals in the connection between the heroism and the tragedy. Do not merely summarize the plot.

2. 'Man has to suffer. When he has no real affliction, he invents some.' Jose Marti, 1853-1895.

   Write about a novel or play in which a central character makes a major contribution to his own suffering. If the character comes to realise that he is responsible in some way for what has happened to him, show how he handles that realisation. How central to the work are the themes of suffering and responsibility?

3. 'Nobody speaks the truth when there is something they must have.' Elizabeth Bowen, Anglo-Irish novelist, 1899-1973

   Select a novel or play in which someone is deceitful in order to get something they want. Trace the course of their deceit (which could be self-deceit) and show how the novelist or dramatist carefully controls the means by which the deceit is uncovered.

4. 'Well, all the plays that I was trying to write … were plays that would grab an audience by the throat and not release them, rather than presenting an emotion which you could observe and walk away from.' Arthur Miller.

   Discuss way in which plays you have studied may 'grab an audience by the throat'.

5. 'A play should give you something to think about. When I see a play and understand it the first time, then I know it can't be much good.' T. S. Eliot.

   Discuss aspects of plays you know well which may puzzle an audience at first but which on reflection add to their value as works of literature.

Commentary 'Help' Pages

Practice Commentary 3

a) What do we learn from this passage about Macbeth's attitude towards Banquo?
o   Afraid of B *(2-3)*
o   Believes B is more 'naturally' kingly *(3)*
o   Acknowledges B's courage *(4)*
o   Acknowledges B's wisdom *(6)*
o   Feels diminished by B *(8-9)*
o   Feels envy *(13)*
o   Resents Banquo, who will benefit from the price M has paid *(18)*
o   Resentment again – and some scorn *(23)*

b) How does Macbeth's style of speech reflect his state of mind?
o   Curt phrase – dismissive of what he has achieved *(1)*
o   Absolute statement *'none but he'* – M's tendency to believe that only one more act of violence will solve all his problems *(8)*
o   Simile *('prophet-like')* – his feeling that he is in the hands of fate *(12)*
o   Images of barrenness – fear that his line will come to an end *(14-15)*
o   Powerful verb *'wrenched'* and scornful phrase *'unlineal hand'*– sense of outrage *(16)*
o   *'filed'* ('defiled') suggests sullied, dirtied – beginning of self-loathing *(18)*
o   Internal anguish – *'rancours'* = bitter taste; *'vessel'* = holy chalice? *(20)*
o   Jewel image – realisation that his soul is precious, and fear that he will lose both it and the chance of an after-life *(21)*
o   Desperation, recklessness *(22-23)*
o   Jumpiness *(23)*

Practice Commentary 4

Sample passage

MALCOLM: With this, there grows

          In <u>my most ill-compos'd affection</u>, such

          A <u>staunchless</u> avarice, that, <u>were I king</u>,

          I should <u>cut off</u> the nobles for their lands,

          Desire <u>his</u> jewels, and <u>this other's</u> house,   5

          And my more-having would be <u>as a sauce</u>

          <u>To make me hunger more,</u> that I should <u>forge</u>

          <u>Quarrels</u> unjust against <u>the good and loyal,</u>

          Destroying them for wealth.

MACDUFF: This avarice

          Sticks deeper, grows with more pernicious root   10

          Than summer-seeming lust; and it hath been

          The sword of our slain kings: yet do not fear;

          Scotland hath foisons to fill up your will,

143

Of your mere own. All these are portable,

With other graces weigh'd.   *15*

MALCOLM: <u>But I have none</u>. The king-becoming graces,

As <u>justice, verity, temperance</u>, stableness,

Bounty, perseverance, mercy , lowliness,

Devotion, patience, courage, fortitude,

<u>I have no relish of them</u>; but abound   *20*

In the division of each several <u>crime</u>,

Acting it <u>many</u> ways. Nay, had I power, I should

<u>Pour the sweet milk of concord, into Hell,</u>

<u>Uproar the universal peace</u>, confound

All <u>unity on earth</u>.

MACDUFF: O Scotland! Scotland!   *25*

MALCOLM: <u>If such a one be fit to govern, speak;</u>

<u>I am as I have spoken</u>.

Guiding question

What methods does Malcolm use to test Macduff?

o   (2) General self-depreciation
o   (3) *'staunchless'* – powerful term to describe something flowing which can not be stopped
o   (3) Paints a vivid picture of what a bad king he would be.
o   (4) *'cut off'*: cold-blooded term
o   (5) Makes his cruelty seem more likely by picturing his victims.
o   (6-7) Food image
o   (7-8) Weapon image (quarrel – fired from a cross-bow)
o   (8) Lets Macduff include himself as a potential victim.
o   (17) Quick to contradict Macduff, in plain terms
o   (17) Gives very long list of virtues (twelve in all) which he does not have.
o   (20) Food image again, carrying on from previous
o   (21) Would be a criminal as well as a sinner, he says.
o   (22) Open-ended term: 'many'
o   (23) Food image – milk as a symbol of peace and harmony
o   (23) Hell image – the hell he would create
o   (24-25) 'universal…unity': linked terms emphasising the fundamental harm he would cause
o   (26-27) Challenges Macduff in simple language.
o   (27) Claims one virtue – truthfulness.

<u>Final Words</u>

IF YOU GOT THROUGH ALL OR MOST OF THAT, WELL DONE!
AND GOOD LUCK WITH ANY EXAM YOU'RE PREPARING FOR…

CPSIA information can be obtained
at www.ICGtesting.com
Printed in the USA
BVHW090908130919
558272BV00023B/302/P

9 781071 216903